PRESENTS

THE FA CARLING PREMIERSHIP
WORLD CUP
STARS

PRESENTS

THE FA CARLING PREMIERSHIP
WORLD CUP
STARS

By BRYON BUTLER and FRANK NICKLIN

STOPWATCH

CONTENTS

Foreword by Mark Hunter,
Marketing Director, Bass Brewers   7

Introduction by Bryon Butler   8-9

'Team-Mate v Team-Mate'
    Club-star v club-star - the duels
    the cup may create   10-15

'Golden Moments'
    Highlights from the qualifying rounds   16-18

Player Profiles - Country by Country
The final countdown   19

England   20
Scotland   42
Belgium   52
Croatia   53
Denmark   54
France   60
Germany   63
Holland   64
Italy   67
Jamaica   70
Nigeria   73
Norway   75
Romania   84
South Africa   86
USA   88
Yugoslavia   89

The World Cup Finals
Who plays who, where and when
and the stadiums   91-95

Glossary
Club-by-club, player-by-player   96

FOREWORD

by Mark Hunter, Marketing Director, Bass Brewers

On behalf of Carling, I welcome you to 'The FA Carling Premiership World Cup Stars'. From Adams to Zola, it covers everything you need to know about the Carling Premiership players who are likely to be taking part in the World Cup this summer.

It is a testament to the Carling Premiership's current status within world football, that Bryon Butler was able to write this book. For when the World Cup kicks-off on 10 June 1998, the Carling Premiership will contribute more players to the tournament than any other international league.

Well over a hundred Carling Premiership players are likely to be involved. A number, of course, will be in the England and Scotland squads, but the majority are from the increasingly influential foreign legion.

Just take a look at some of the 45 overseas stars from 14 countries featured in this publication: Di Matteo, Zola, Bergkamp, Overmars, Klinsmann, Bilic, Schmeichel...the list of world-class players goes on and on.

Add these to the home grown stars that Glenn Hoddle and Craig Brown have at their disposal and it's easy to see why the Carling Premiership is the world's most exciting club competition. But the best is set to get better! Who knows

how many more stars will come to this country after the World Cup has finished?

Let us hope the England and Scotland teams maintain the excellent form they showed in qualification and that both can progress to the latter stages.

Vive Le Football!

Mark Hunter

PLAYER AWARDS: 1994 – 1998

As the list below illustrates, a large number of the previous winners of the Carling Player of the Month Award are featured in this book, others have now retired, while some will feature in future World Cups. However, one thing they all have in common is the starring role they've played in making the Carling Premiership the world's most exciting club competition!

Carling Player Awards - 1994/95	Carling Player Awards - 1995/96	Carling Player Awards - 1996/97	Carling Player Awards - 1997/98
Aug Jurgen Klinsmann	**Aug** David Ginola	**Aug** David Beckham	**(to date)**
Sept Robert Lee	**Sept** Tony Yeboah	**Sept** Patrik Berger	**Aug** Dennis Bergkamp
Oct Paul Ince	**Oct** Trevor Sinclair	**Oct** Matt Le Tissier	**Sept** Dennis Bergkamp
Nov Chris Sutton/Alan Shearer	**Nov** Robert Lee	**Nov** Ian Wright	**Oct** Paulo Wanchope
Dec Matt Le Tissier	**Dec** Robbie Fowler	**Dec** Gianfranco Zola	**Nov** Andy Cole/Kevin Davies
Jan Chris Waddle	**Jan** Robbie Fowler/Stan Collymore	**Jan** Tim Flowers	**Dec** Steve McManaman
Feb Duncan Ferguson	**Feb** Dwight Yorke	**Feb** Robbie Earle	**Jan** Dion Dublin
Mar Tony Yeboah	**Mar** Eric Cantona	**Mar** Juninho	**Feb** Chris Sutton
Apr David Seaman	**Apr** Andrei Kanchelskis	**Apr** Mickey Evans	
Carling Player of the Year	Carling Player of the Year	Carling Player of the Year	
Alan Shearer	**Peter Schmeichel**	**Juninho**	

*Stade Velodrome, Marseilles -
scene of England's first game*

INTRODUCTION

A cumulative television audience of 37 billion people - or, more awesomely, 37,000,000,000 - will watch the 16th finals of the World Cup in France. The eggheads who worked this out probably practised their counting on the stars in the sky or the grains of sand on a beach. The figure is too big to grasp.

It is a gallery which confirms that the World Cup is the greatest prize in all sport. Nothing absorbs this cosmic speck more than the battle to decide who is cleverest and strongest at directing a ball into a net.

No national league in football, however, will be making a greater contribution to this high summit of the game than the FA Carling Premiership. Around 160 foreigners are employed by the 20 clubs of the Carling Premiership; and a sovereign percentage of them will be in France - which adds a brand new dimension to home interest in the finals.

England and Scotland, yes, of course...but Manchester United fan's will also be rooting for Peter Schmeichel of Denmark and their Norwegian stars. Chelsea supporters will take pride in the performances of Gianfranco Zola and Roberto di Matteo of Italy. Arsenal's disciples will be watching Holland closely. Wimbledon and Derby County will have a soft spot for Jamaica, and other Carling Premiership eyes will be on Germany, South Africa, the United States, Nigeria, Romania and the rest. Familiar faces in different colours on a bigger stage - plus, interestingly, those who have come and gone, Asprilla, Ravenelli and their like.

The FA Carling Premiership has become almost a 'Who's Who?' of the international set, a honeypot for talent from all over the globe, and has played its part in making England's championship perhaps the most exciting,

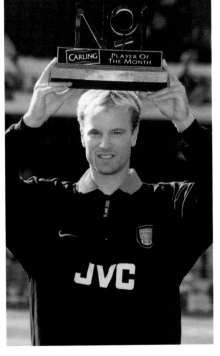

most colourful and most successful of all. English football has always had a high opinion of itself - but its pride in the Carling Premiership is justified.

The League's foreigners are handsomely paid, but, in return, they have sharpened standards, introduced new ideas and techniques and even changed the shape and tempo of English football. They have stimulated and graced the game, heightened expectations and raised the level of entertainment. Some, of course, have made an infinitely bigger impact than others. Some

have openly admitted that the rigours of the Carling Premiership have improved their own skills and attitudes.

More, too, will be on the way after these World Cup finals. The tournament will be a huge shop window for the players involved - and quality and character will be studied closely by English club managers as well as the coaches and agents of Italy and the rest.

Football's market place may have lost some of its sanity - it could be argued that it's never had all its marbles - but there's no going back. The pursuit of success, or at least the need to look ambitious, means that the big clubs of Europe must continue to spend...even if they can't afford to.

But the buying and selling will come later. Only the game itself will matter between June 10 and July 12. A record entry of 172 countries played 643 qualifying games over nearly two years to decide which 30 of them would join Brazil, the holders, and France, the hosts, in this summer's big dog-fight. And in 33 days another 64 games will be played in ten stadiums before one nation is acclaimed as the football champions of planet Earth.

This book identifies most of the Carling Premiership men who have played a significant role in guiding their countries to France - plus most of the certainties and many of the probables and possibles for the finals themselves. We wish them well... let the party begin.

TEAM-MATE V
TEAM-MATE

Friend or Foe? That will be the burning question when Carling Premiership team-mates of different nationalities come face to face in World Cup 1998. Here we team up a few of the possible clashes as the tournament progresses.

GRAEME LE SAUX and DAN PETRESCU

Graeme Le Saux and Dan Petrescu, both combatant Chelsea regulars, have the Bridge fans licking their lips in anticipation of the first crunching challenge when England meet Romania on June 22.

TONY ADAMS and DENNIS BERGKAMP

*A*rsenal fans will be eyeing the prospect of Tony Adams and Dennis Bergkamp in opposition if England and Holland make it to the quarter-finals.

GUNNAR HALLE and DAVID HOPKIN

*W*hen David Hopkin goes wading in for the Scots against Norway on June 16, he will not expect a cheery welcome from his Leeds clubmate in the opposition defence.

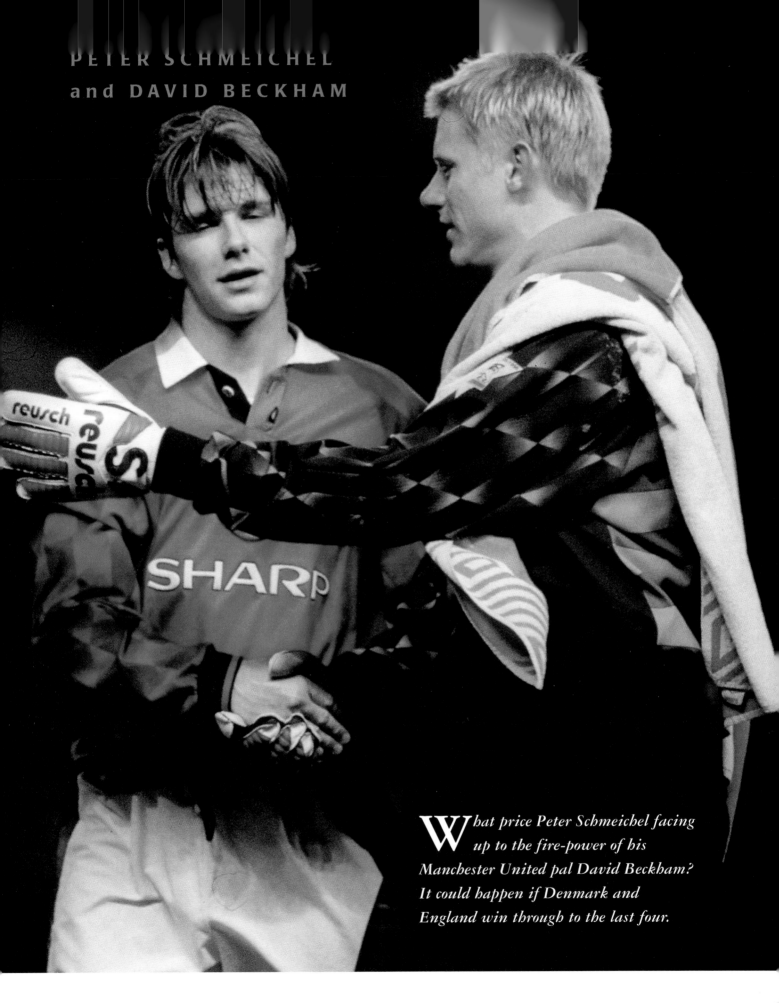

PETER SCHMEICHEL
and DAVID BECKHAM

What price Peter Schmeichel facing up to the fire-power of his Manchester United pal David Beckham? It could happen if Denmark and England win through to the last four.

MARK FISH and PER FRANDSEN

I nstead of friend or foe, it will be Fish or Frandsen in Toulouse on the afternoon of June 18, that's when Bolton's stalwarts from South Africa and Denmark meet in the first round.

PAUL INCE and OYVIND LEONHARDSEN

Liverpool team-mates Paul Ince and Oyvind Leonhardsen on opposite sides is an interesting thought. It will be for real if England and Norway meet in the semi-finals.

JURGEN KLINSMANN and SOL CAMPBELL

The very real possibility of England and Germany meeting at some stage, a game to be savoured, suggests the fascinating scenario of Sol Campbell v Jurgen Klinsmann. Tottenham fans can hardly wait.

GOLDEN MOMENTS

The road to France began on March 10, 1996 with Dominica v Antigua. Twenty months and some 650 qualifying matches later, a mere 32 nations have emerged triumphant. They are the lucky ones still on cloud nine with memories of golden goals and nail-biting finishes. Here, from the bulging scrapbooks of those magic moments, we present action replays of a few that meant so much for the Carling Premiership stars involved. And with so many in action with their national sides, this has to be the most exciting and the most thrill-packed close season in the history of the Carling Premiership!

Viorel Moldovan, Coventry's new pride and joy, almost on target for Romania against the Republic of Ireland. The result was 1-1, the only qualifier Romania didn't win.

The world belongs to Colin Hendry of Blackburn as Scotland beat Latvia 2-0 to clinch the best runners-up qualifying spot.

Alan Shearer celebrates after scoring in the 2-0 victory over Georgia at Wembley.

Happiness is a goalless draw for England's heroes David Seaman and the bloodstained Paul Ince in the vital Rome qualifier with Italy.

This was the moment when Italian cheers echoed across Wembley. The scorer is Gianfranco Zola, despite the despairing lunge of his London club rival Sol Campbell, and England have lost 0-1.

Savo Milosevic took time off from Villa Park to notch this goal for Yugoslavia in the 7-1 humiliation of Hungary in their play-off match.

Here's a picture familiar to Manchester United fans, but this time it's Peter Schmeichel celebrating Denmark's 2-0 defeat of Bosnia.

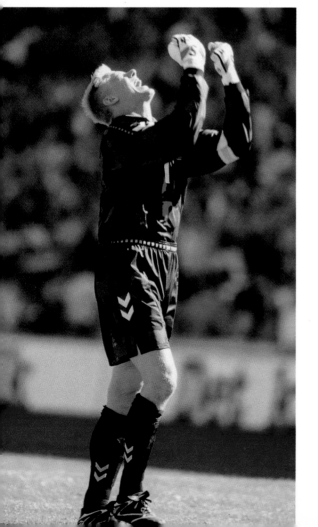

Norway have just qualified! Hence the melon-slice smiles of the Leeds United twosome, Gunnar Halle and Alf-Inge Haaland, after beating Switzerland 5-0 to remain unbeaten and head the group.

ENGLAND

Michel Platini, once a great player and now head of the France 98 organising machine, said of Glenn Hoddle that had he been a Frenchman, he would have won 150 caps. In fact, he had 53 senior games and 12 under-21 games for England. The plus side is that Hoddle is now applying with great success his rare skills and imagination as national coach. The supreme reward may yet be his.

England's World Cup history is topsy-turvy. They have played in nine finals, won it once, died gloriously in another semi-final on penalties to West Germany, and failed pathetically three times even to qualify. Their 1998 qualifying record on a hard, stony trail was commendable, despite the Wembley blip against Italy. Nobody should rate Moldova, Georgia and Poland as pushovers; the ultimate 0-0 in Rome was England's and Hoddle's finest hour.

Ungenerously, unseeded England are quoted in the shops around 6-1, even with the canny Hoddle and a fighting fit Shearer in command. Encouragingly, not a single turnip has yet been thrown by the equally ungenerous tabloids.

DAVID SEAMAN
ARSENAL

An England goalkeeper in the regal tradition of Gordon Banks, Peter Shilton and Ray Clemence. Seaman is a modest and uncomplicated son of Rotherham, an exemplary professional and one of the most popular figures in English football. A big bear of an athlete with safe hands, canny judgement of angles and distance and sharp reflexes. Organises defences well, has no apparent caution or doubt in his game and is as likely as any 'keeper to save a penalty. Seaman was one of the heroes of Euro 96 and captained his country against Moldova on the way to France - only the sixth goalkeeper to lead England.

He has even been described as the best in Europe - but he has never forgotten the day 17 years ago, when, as an apprentice with Leeds, he was told he wasn't going to make it. "Whatever I've achieved since then" he says "is the result of hard work". He has helped Arsenal to win the championship, FA Cup, League Cup and European Cup Winners' Cup to prove that sweat pays.

DAVID SEAMAN	
V I T A L S T A T I S T I C S	
Born	19.3.63. Rotherham
Height	6'4"
Weight	14-10
Previous clubs	Leeds United, Peterborough United, Birmingham City, QPR
1998 World Cup Qualifiers	7 (Mol, Pol, Geo, Geo, Pol, Mol, Ita)

NIGEL MARTYN

LEEDS UNITED

Cornishmen are a proud lot and with some justification. They are very good at fishing, mining, Rugby Union, pasties and holidays for people from lesser places. They have not, however, contributed much to the history of football - which is something Martyn would like to help put right. He was born in St Austell, a few days after England's World Cup success in 1966, and, by way of Bristol Rovers and Crystal Palace, he is now recognised as one of the best in his eccentric trade. Leeds paid a record £2.25 million for him (one more high-water mark for Cornwall) and considered they had a bargain. Martyn is a powerful and imposing chap with safe hands, athletic movement, sound judgement and bags of courage.

NIGEL MARTYN

VITAL STATISTICS

Born	11.8.66. St Austell
Height	6'1"
Weight	14-7
Previous Clubs	Bristol Rovers, Crystal Palace

IAN WALKER
TOTTENHAM HOTSPUR

Walker took a hammering from the media after Gianfranco Zola had squeezed in Italy's winner against England at Wembley early in 1997. It was unfair because England had been undermined in all areas of the field; but, then, goalkeepers are not allowed the odd mistake. Walker must also have wished sometimes that he had a stronger defence in front of him at White Hart Lane, but it is a measure of the man that he continues to manage saves that he has no right to make. He has fast reflexes, positive control of his area and is always prepared to dive in where it might hurt. His father, Mike, now the manager of Norwich, was also a goalkeeper.

IAN WALKER
VITAL STATISTICS

Born	31.10.71. Watford
Height	6'2"
Weight	13-1
Previous clubs	Oxford United (loan) Ipswich Town (loan)
1998 World Cup qualifiers	1 (Ita)

MARTIN KEOWN
ARSENAL

Keown plays every game as if it is the biggest of his life and the last of his career - a life which began during the 1966 World Cup and a career which has lasted 13 years and taken him from Arsenal to Arsenal by way of Aston Villa and Everton. He moved back to Highbury from Goodison Park for £2 million five years ago and, quietly but doggedly, has established himself as a defender who can be trusted. His early role as a Jack-of-all-trades, anywhere in defence or mid-field, rather undermined his progress; but now it is accepted that he is at his best as a marker and spoiler in central defence. He is sharp and res-olute but always calm and always a team-man. He talks as good a game as he plays – but has had rotten luck with injuries.

MARTIN KEOWN	
VITAL STATISTICS	
Born	24.7.66. Oxford
Height	6'1"
Weight	12-4
Previous clubs	Arsenal, Brighton (loan), Aston Villa, Everton

GARETH SOUTHGATE
ASTON VILLA

Yes, he missed that penalty at the sharp end of Euro 96; but legendary hitmen such as Pele, Platini, Rush and Lineker have also bumbled things from the spot. Southgate is a modern centre-back who deserves to be remembered more for his intelligence, ability to smother trouble and inventiveness in promoting attacks. His friendliness with the ball is explained by the fact that he was a midfielder with Crystal Palace before joining Aston Villa for £2.5 million in the summer of 1995. The wisdom of the move was soon confirmed by club and country, and he was at his best, significantly, against Dennis Bergkamp and Holland at Wembley during Euro 96. Southgate is a keen student and articulate observer of the game who, one day, should make a good manager or media man.

GARETH SOUTHGATE	
V I T A L S T A T I S T I C S	
Born	3.9.70. Watford
Height	6'0"
Weight	12-3
Previous club	Crystal Palace
1998 World Cup qualifiers	7 (Mol, Pol, Geo, Geo - sub, Pol, Mol, Ita)

SOL CAMPBELL
TOTTENHAM HOTSPUR

Campbell has such size and presence that he seems to fill his penalty area: opponents have to make a long detour to avoid him. He took some time to settle down with Spurs and England but he now looks immovable - someone who could stand perfectly still in the face of a typhoon. He played in most positions while he was learning the game and it was Gerry Francis, at White Hart Lane, who decided he had been created to be a centre-back.

Campbell is flexible, undentable and, despite his size, bitingly quick. He is also unflappable and, season by season, is moving out of defence with increasing authority. His eye for options is also getting sharper. He is 23 and readily admits he is learning from every experience - including the moment when Gianfranco Zola breezed past him to score Italy's winner at Wembley.

SOL CAMPBELL	
V I T A L S T A T I S T I C S	
Born	18.9.74. Newham
Height	6'2"
Weight	14-4
1998 World Cup qualifiers	6 (Geo, Ita, Geo, Pol, Mol, Ita)

TONY ADAMS
ARSENAL

Arsenal's captain is everyone's idea of a proper England centre-half: roof-top tall, a bully in the air, a destroyer on the ground, a marker who can squeeze between an opponent and his after-shave and a spirited adventurer when opportunity beckons. He has a fighter's face, with lantern jaw and impassive eyes, and a character that is decidedly crusty. He has been at the heart of Arsenal's defence for more than a decade,

but the demands of English football are catching up with him physically. He was in commanding form for England during Euro 96 despite a knee problem which required pain-killing injections - and his list of injuries during the Nineties make painful reading. His biggest problem, though, has been himself. He has faced his drink addiction with courage and his private life has been a matter for him, occasionally the law and, from time to time, a few million newspaper readers. On the field, however, he has proved himself one of England's outstanding defenders.

TONY ADAMS
VITAL STATISTICS

Born	10.10.66. London
Height	6'3"
Weight	13-11
1998 World Cup qualifiers	3 (Geo, Geo, Ita)

GRAEME LE SAUX
CHELSEA

Who and what is a 'typical' footballer? Well, Le Saux is - and he isn't. He is intelligent, articulate, polite, loves music and is his own man; but that can be said of many others. Le Saux, however, has an image which sets him slightly apart, one of the chaps but not laddish, someone who keeps things in perspective and jibs at admitting that football is the most important thing in his life. But, that said, he plays it uncommonly well. He is a wing-back or left-back who is creative, determined an always looking to introduce and element of surprise.

Le Saux, brought up in Jersey, moved from Chelsea to Blackburn, won a championship medal and sustained a horrible ankle injury which kept him out of the game for ten months, and then returned to Chelsea last August. He moved north for £500,000 and back south for £5 million. Gives credit for the best of his football education to Terry Venables and Kenny Dalglish. Deserves top marks himself for attitude and courage.

GRAEME LE SAUX

VITAL STATISTICS

Born	17.10.68. Jersey
Height	5'10"
Weight	12-2
Previous clubs	Chelsea, Blackburn Rovers
1998 World Cup qualifiers	4 (Ita, Geo, Pol, Ita)

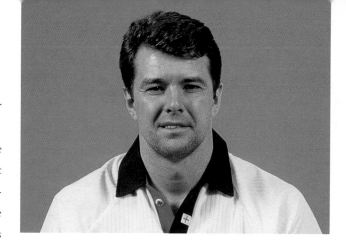

GARY PALLISTER
MANCHESTER UNITED

A towering cornerstone of United's defence throughout the Nineties, and he would have won more caps for England but for injuries. He gives the impression he would head cannon-balls and tackle charging rhinos if necessary. His experience gives him an answer to most problems and his consistency is a source of confidence to fellow defenders.

Pallister's beginnings, however, were unusual and uncertain. He was on the dole and playing non-League football when he was spotted by Middlesborough who then loaned him to Darlington. But his very obvious qualities soon meant he was one of the most talked about young defenders in the country, and Alex Ferguson was happy to pay a hefty £2.3 million for him in August 1989. Since when, he has acquired an enviable collection of winners' medals. "Sometimes" he admits "I have to wonder whether it's all really happened."

GARY PALLISTER	
V I T A L S T A T I S T I C S	
Born	30.8.65. Ramsgate
Height	6'4"
Weight	15-0
Previous clubs	Middlesbrough, Darlington (loan)
1998 World Cup qualifiers	2 (Mol, Pol - sub)

RIO FERDINAND
WEST HAM UNITED

One for the future. Ferdinand is only 19 but he has received so much praise that it can only be hoped he has the strength of character to do justice to all the expectations and his own rich talent. He has played in many positions, including striker, but his future is in central defence, a job he does with polished technique and rare touch, awareness and vision, a destroyer and creator with all the right instincts in one tall and slender package. He might have won his first England cap against Moldova last September, but a drink-driver incident saw him dropped abruptly from the squad. But he did not have to wait long for his chance. He was sent on as a second-half substitute for Gareth Southgate against Cameroon two months later. He is a bright young man and says simply: "Mistakes can be worthwhile if you learn from them". He is a distant cousin of Les Ferdinand.

RIO FERDINAND	
V I T A L S T A T I S T I C S	
Born	7.11.78. Peckham
Height	6'2"
Weight	12-0
Previous clubs	Bournemouth (loan)

GARY NEVILLE	
VITAL STATISTICS	
Born	18.2.75. Bury
Height	5'11"
Weight	12-4
1998 World Cup qualifiers	6 (Mol, Pol, Ita, Geo, Mol, Pol)

back, Phil on both flanks. And both have excellent temperaments, handle pressure well and pick things up quickly. Terry Venables has said that Gary could even develop into an England captain. The Neville brothers are as level-headed off the field as on it - a credit to their father, Neville Neville, who is Bury's commercial manager.

GARY & PHIL NEVILLE
MANCHESTER UNITED

The first brothers to play in the same England side since the Charltons - their first caps together in the game against China in Beijing in May 1996.

Gary is the older one, by two years, and also the noisier. Phil, insist some, is the more naturally gifted but has been unluckier with injury and illness. Both are modern, adaptable defenders: Gary has played at wing-back and centre-

PHIL NEVILLE	
VITAL STATISTICS	
Born	21.1.77. Bury
Height	5'11"
Weight	11-10
1998 World Cup qualifiers	2 (Pol - sub, Mol)

DAVID BATTY
NEWCASTLE UNITED

Batty is a 'pro's pro' which means, among other things, that most players would prefer to play with him rather than against him. He is essentially a midfield-anchor but the description 'hard man' does him less than justice. He was one of England's outstanding players against Italy in Rome, a night which demanded more than muscular competence.

Batty is a flint-faced middleweight who wins the ball and then passes it without flourish or posture. His tackles count, just as the butt of a bull counts, which means he is on close terms with most referees. Not a play-maker, but certainly a man who allows and persuades others to play. Not a greyhound, but he never stops running. He plays to his considerable strengths.

A championship winner with Leeds and Blackburn and one day, he believes, with Newcastle as well. He is also convinced England can win the World Cup. He has confidence to spare.

NICKY BUTT
MANCHESTER UNITED

One more of Old Trafford's outstanding graduates; and perhaps the fastest improving of them all. A young tiger who can play box-to-box or, his most effective role, a holder and liaison man between sentries and raiders. Butt has tremendous vitality, a wisdom beyond his years and is always involved. He has worked hard on his game, particularly his passing, and Alex Ferguson, United's manager, has frequently made a point of praising his performances. "I think Nicky will get even better as he matures" he says. "He just keeps on learning and adding new dimensions to his game". And, like most of Ferguson's young men, Butt handles the trappings of fame with a level head.

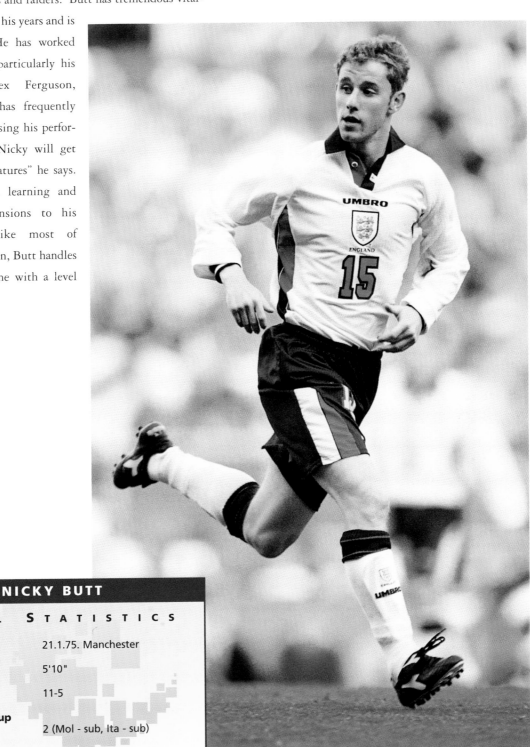

NICKY BUTT

VITAL STATISTICS

Born	21.1.75. Manchester
Height	5'10"
Weight	11-5
1998 World Cup qualifiers	2 (Mol - sub, Ita - sub)

DAVID BECKHAM
MANCHESTER UNITED

Beckham has travelled so far and fast in the past three years that it is difficult to imagine where he might be in another three years time. An informed guess would be somewhere over the moon. But his profile, even at that height, would be unmistakable. Not every footballer scores goals from 50 yards in the Premiership or is engaged to one of the Spice girls.

Beckham looked outstanding as a kid since when, a question of promise fulfilled, he has got bigger and wiser. He strikes the ball beautifully, his range and accuracy can turn a match and he is always willing to try something different. He is also modest, but not over-modest, personable, professional, ambitious.....and still has at least another ten years at the top.

DAVID BECKHAM
VITAL STATISTICS

Born	2.5.75. Leytonstone
Height	6'0"
Weight	11-12
1998 World Cup qualifiers	8 (Mol, Pol, Geo, Ita, Geo, Pol, Mol, Ita)

PAUL SCHOLES
MANCHESTER UNITED

Scholes is 23-years-old, 5ft 7ins tall, modest and has suffered from asthma - and, says Glenn Hoddle, he could be England's "jewel in the crown" in France. Scholes, well proportioned, balanced and ferret-quick, has had only four seasons in the Premiership; but his maturity already gives point to a talent which Hoddle describes as "immense". Scholes fits readily into any team-pattern, central or wide midfield, or as a secondary striker, and he finishes potently with either foot. His goal against Cameroon, taken with a moment's check and then a calculated chip, is just one example - a little gem. Scholes learnt much from Eric Cantona at Old Trafford and further experience on the high plateau of the game could see him become a major player of long term significance.

PAUL SCHOLES

VITAL STATISTICS

Born	16.11.74. Salford
Height	5'7"
Weight	11-8
1998 World Cup qualifiers	1 (Mol)
Goals	1 (Mol)

PAUL INCE
LIVERPOOL

Ince is stuck with one image above all: the one portrayed by that picture of him, forehead bloodied and bandaged, after England's crucial draw against Italy in Rome. He may well be a loving family man and a wag in the dressing room; but he is regarded as a noisy and fractious fistful - a *talented*, noisy and fractious fistful - on the park. Just the sort of player managers love, of course, which is why he was able to leave West Ham and earn loads of money with Manchester United, Inter Milan and Liverpool. He has styled himself the "Guv'nor" and, indeed, is the first black player to have captained England. His all-round game has been broadened and sharpened by his travels, and his combativeness is now enriched by greater craft and all-round vision.

PAUL INCE	
V I T A L S T A T I S T I C S	
Born	21.10.67. Ilford
Height	5'10"
Weight	11-7
Previous clubs	West Ham Utd, Manchester Utd, Internationale Milan (Italy)
1998 World Cup qualifiers	7 (Mol, Pol, Geo, Ita, Geo, Pol, Ita)

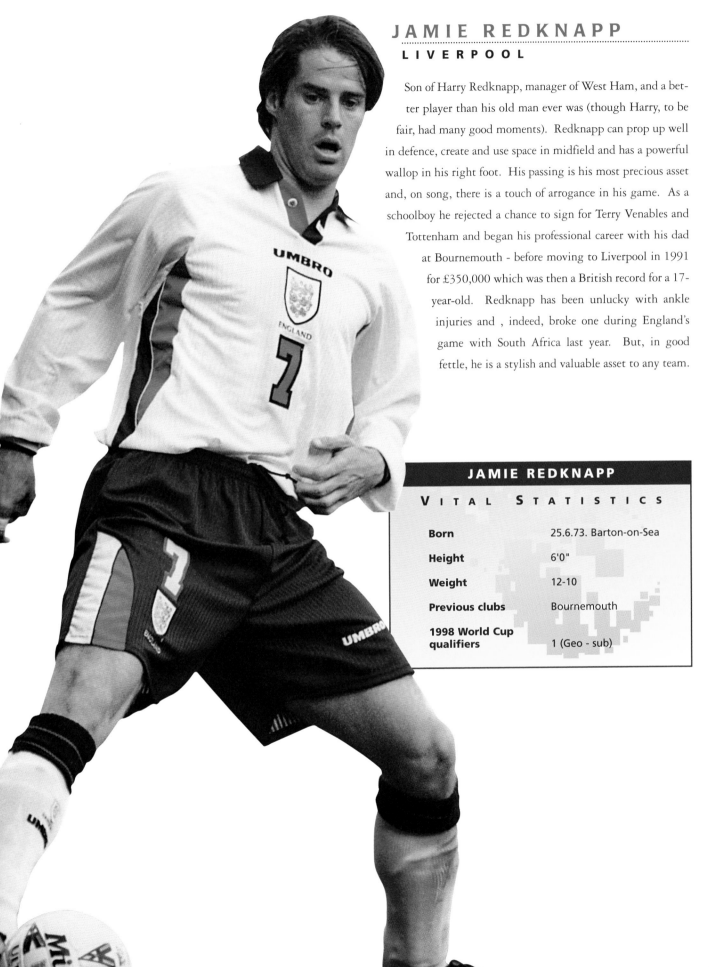

JAMIE REDKNAPP
LIVERPOOL

Son of Harry Redknapp, manager of West Ham, and a better player than his old man ever was (though Harry, to be fair, had many good moments). Redknapp can prop up well in defence, create and use space in midfield and has a powerful wallop in his right foot. His passing is his most precious asset and, on song, there is a touch of arrogance in his game. As a schoolboy he rejected a chance to sign for Terry Venables and Tottenham and began his professional career with his dad at Bournemouth - before moving to Liverpool in 1991 for £350,000 which was then a British record for a 17-year-old. Redknapp has been unlucky with ankle injuries and , indeed, broke one during England's game with South Africa last year. But, in good fettle, he is a stylish and valuable asset to any team.

JAMIE REDKNAPP
VITAL STATISTICS

Born	25.6.73. Barton-on-Sea
Height	6'0"
Weight	12-10
Previous clubs	Bournemouth
1998 World Cup qualifiers	1 (Geo - sub)

ANDY COLE
MANCHESTER UNITED

Cole, fit and hungry, is back on the high plateau of the game. He scattered Newcastle scoring records to the four winds and then, amid much hullabaloo three years ago, moved from the big-time to the even bigger time with Manchester United for around £7 million. Injuries, illness and loss of confidence raised doubts about the investment and his future. But Eric Cantona left Old Trafford, Teddy Sheringham arrived and Cole has identified himself again as one of English football's most dangerous hit-men - a player, says Alex Ferguson, who is "different".

Cole's speed is pantherish, his instincts are unpredictable and he links well inside and outside the box. He demands close attention and is clever at drawing and shifting markers. An expert lurker.

ANDY COLE	
VITAL STATISTICS	
Born	15.10.71. Nottingham
Height	5'10"
Weight	12-1
Previous clubs	Arsenal, Fulham (loan), Bristol City, Newcastle United

TEDDY SHERINGHAM
MANCHESTER UNITED

There are those in football who say Sheringham is too slow - which begs a question: How good would this man be if he could move from 0-60 mph in about the time it takes to spell his name? The more important fact is that Sheringham is one of the quickest thinkers in English football which, allied to touch and vision, gives him an important edge in most company. He scores goals with head or either foot, many of high quality, but he also oils the machinery around him. He involves others and, for England, has bonded strongly with Alan Shearer.

He is tall and straight, with a hint of an old Corinthian about him, but he is always up with the tempo and patterns of the modern game. He left Millwall because they weren't big enough and then moved from Nottingham Forest to Tottenham because he was ambitious - only to discover that even Spurs were marking time. So, like cream, he rose to the top with Manchester United and is proving he is good enough to fill the gap left by Eric Cantona.

TEDDY SHERINGHAM	
VITAL STATISTICS	
Born	2.4.66. Highams Park
Height	6'0"
Weight	12-8
Previous clubs	Millwall, Aldershot (loan), Nottingham Forest, Tottenham Hotspur
1998 World Cup qualifiers	4 (Geo, Geo, Pol, Ita)
Goals	3 (Geo, Geo, Pol)

STEVE McMANAMAN

LIVERPOOL

When Pele speaks, we listen; and Pele says that McManaman can be compared with George Best the great Brazilian doesn't always get things right, but it is certainly true that the lanky Liverpool illusionist is a pulse-stirring entertainer and a very effective player. McManaman on the move, making one of his puncturing runs, body taut and angular, sends out all kinds of messages - particularly to opposing defenders and watching supporters. His severe control and evasive changes of pace and direction are murder to stop and fun to watch. And, after criticism earlier in his career, he'd also finishing with more accuracy and courage. A goal-of-the-month spectacular is always on the agenda.

McManaman doesn't do it every match (not even Best did) but wherever he plays, wide or free agent, he is perceived to be a potential match-winner. He is often paid the pretty compliment of a personal marker - and he also happens to be a bright and stylish chap who enjoys a jokey night out and writes a column for a very serious newspaper.

STEVE McMANAMAN	
VITAL STATISTICS	
Born	11.2.72. Liverpool
Height	6'0"
Weight	10-6
1998 World Cup qualifiers	2 (Pol, Ita)

ALAN SHEARER
NEWCASTLE UNITED

Shearer, contrary to many knowledgeable sources, is just a human being who bleeds when he is cut and hurts when he is kicked; and, just to emphasise the point, he has sustained some nasty injuries, cruciate ligament, groin, hernia, etc etc. England had to rub along without him during their final push towards France - but their chances of winning the World Cup will be immeasurably enhanced if he is on song during the finals.

So much is always expected of Shearer; but it is a mark of the man that he is always likely to exceed expectations. He is, in short, a striker with just about everything. He is technically complete, strong of mind and body, nerveless and focussed and selfless, a dreadnought who is never intimidated or subdued and a marksman who can produce the right kind of strike to order. Yes, he did go 12 internationals without a goal but, when it mattered, he was the leading scorer in Euro 96. His story, of course, is well documented. Southampton to Blackburn for a British record fee, a championship, Blackburn to home-town Newcastle for a world record fee of £15 million, the captaincy of England and goals and awards all the way.

ALAN SHEARER	
VITAL STATISTICS	
Born	13.8.70. Newcastle
Height	5'11"
Weight	12-6
Previous clubs	Southampton, Blackburn Rovers
1998 World Cup qualifiers	5 (Mol, Pol, Ita, Geo, Pol)
Goals	5 (Mol, Pol 2, Geo, Pol)

IAN WRIGHT

ARSENAL

One of the sharpest bayonets in English football, a sinewy, ebony-muscled pillager who is fast enough to nobble a dragonfly and scorer of the kind of extrovert goals which test the upper register of commentators. He is Arsenal's record goalscorer and David Seaman, his Highbury colleague, says "he makes it so hard for goalkeepers because he's so unpredictable and comes at you so quickly. You don't know whether he's going to chip you, shoot early or go around you". Wright admits that sometimes he doesn't even see the goalkeeper.

But, says his former Arsenal manager, George Graham, "you have to take Ian warts and all" - and Wright himself has confessed he is "a certified show-off, people love me or hate me". He has been regularly disciplined for out-of-order remarks and gestures and misbehaviour. The style is the man: he often feels "misunderstood". But, at 34, he is still playing and celebrating like a hyper-active boy in a playground - though his fitness problems are increasing.

IAN WRIGHT	
V I T A L S T A T I S T I C S	
Born	3.11.63. Woolwich
Height	5'9"
Weight	11-8
Previous clubs	Crystal Palace
1998 World Cup qualifiers	4 (Geo - sub, Ita - sub, Mol, Ita)
Goals	2 (Mol 2)

MICHAEL OWEN
LIVERPOOL

Owen is in his first full season at the top but has looked a star for the past three years - and he became the youngest England International this century when he played in the friendly against Chile in February at the age of 18 years and 59 days. He is a diamond from Chester who has scored goals at every level, from the England schoolboys' team upwards, with great panache and almost monotonous regularity. His speed and sting are killers and he has exactly the right kind of temperament, and the necessary levels of determination and commitment, to make the most of his talent. He is still learning the game, still learning when and where to go and how to turn errors to his advantage, but this simply means he is going to become even better. Owen was once sent off in an England Under-18 game against Yugoslavia for butting ("A silly thing to do...I just blew up with frustration") but this lapse apart, his attitude to the game is beyond reproach. "At the top level you get a lot of punishment" he says "but you have to live with it."

MICHAEL OWEN	
VITAL STATISTICS	
Born	14.12.79. Chester
Height	5'8"
Weight	10-7

SCOTLAND

Scotland's unbroken history of World Cup failure could be about to end in France. That is the considered opinion of Craig Brown, a coach not renowned for pre-match hysteria.

His optimism is born of the consistency and notable team spirit - both too often lacking in their seven finals appearances - which has deservedly earned the Scots their qualification as best runners-up in the nine European groups.

They were beaten only once in ten qualifying matches, 2-1 in Sweden, and took four points from Austria, the ultimate group winners. They had the best defensive record, conceding only three goals, and found inspiration in their lively striker Kevin Gallacher, who scored six.

A further plus for Brown is the probable 'backroom' help from Walter Smith, the retiring Rangers' manager. The pair assisted Alex Ferguson at Mexico 1986, when they lost narrowly to Denmark and West Germany and held Uruguay to a draw.

Although they have never beaten Brazil, Scotland treasure the memory of a goalless draw against the defending champions in 1974 under the inspiring leadership of Billy Bremner. Another 0-0 on the afternoon of June 10, 1998, will do nicely.

NEIL SULLIVAN
WIMBLEDON

Sullivan is one of that increasingly rare species, the one club player although, strictly speaking, he did play one League game for Crystal Palace while on loan to them. He was born at Sutton, in Surrey, and is a product of Wimbledon's youth scheme - a powerful man who is now recognised as one of the most consistent goalkeepers in the Premiership. He had injury problems early on but, since establishing himself, he has become noted for determination and command of his penalty area. He can be an inspired shot-stopper, has a good record with penalties and is cool under pressure. His grandfather was born in Glasgow.

NEIL SULLIVAN
VITAL STATISTICS

Born	24.2.70. Sutton
Height	6'0"
Weight	12-1
Previous club	Crystal Palace (loan)

MATT ELLIOTT
LEICESTER CITY

Elliott is a latecomer to the big stage but is making up for lost time. He played for Epsom and Ewell, Charlton, Torquay, Scunthorpe and Oxford United before reaching Leicester and the Premiership early in 1997, but he is now respected by every striker in the country. Tall and powerful, he commands the airwaves, tackles swiftly and sharply, looks after himself when the going gets tough and, with foot or head, is a formidable contributor to set-pieces. He was born in London but has a Scottish grandmother and played his first game for Scotland against France in St Etienne last November.

MATT ELLIOTT	
VITAL STATISTICS	
Born	1.11.68. Roehampton
Height	6'3"
Weight	14-10
Previous clubs	Charlton Athletic, Torquay United, Scunthorpe United, Oxford United

CHRISTIAN DAILLY

DERBY COUNTY

Dailly's ability has never been much of a secret. He was only 16 when he made the first of his record number of appearances for Scotland's Under-21 side. But his progress for Dundee United and Derby, whom he joined in the summer of 1996, was noted by many - including Craig Brown who gave him his first full cap last May. Dailly is a versatile type. He began in midfield but central defence is now considered his best position, a job he tackles with steely authority and uncomplicated method. He broke his jaw in December but now, once again, he is proving that he is one of Scotland's new tide of young talent.

CHRISTIAN DAILLY

VITAL STATISTICS

Born	23.10.73. Dundee
Height	6'0"
Weight	12-6
Previous club	Dundee United
1998 World Cup qualifiers	3 (Bel, Bel, Lat)

COLIN CALDERWOOD
TOTTENHAM HOTSPUR

Calderwood is a battle-hardened realist. "Football" he says "is not always as beautiful to play as some people imagine". He speaks as a central defender who is in regular and painful touch with the heads, boots, knees and elbows of the Premiership's most aggressive hitmen. Calderwood, however, stands up well to the social demands of life in the penalty area. He is strong and reliable, tackles with weighty conviction and concedes nothing in the air. Just occasionally, too, he likes to link up in attack.

Calderwood was Ossie Ardiles' first signing for Tottenham in 1993, moving for £1.25 million from Swindon - where he was impressed and improved by Glenn Hoddle.

COLIN CALDERWOOD	
VITAL STATISTICS	
Born	20.1.65. Glasgow
Height	6'0"
Weight	13-0
Previous clubs	Mansfield Town, Swindon Town
1998 World Cup qualifiers	9 (Aus, Lat, Swe, Est, Est, Aus, Swe, Bel, Lat)

BILLY McKINLAY
BLACKBURN ROVERS

A flinty competitor with a sledgehammer tackle who, not altogether surprisingly, has regular brushes with authority. Last season he was booked 13 times. But McKinlay is more than just a licensed bouncer. His involvement in midfield is total, he takes weight off his defence and is a springboard for incisive attacks. He used to score more goals during his eight years with Dundee United whom he left for £1.75 million in 1995 after turning down a chance to join Celtic. There was a time at Blackburn when his career seemed to be faltering, but then there were changes at the top and his star has risen again.

BILLY McKINLAY

VITAL STATISTICS

Born	22.4.69. Glasgow
Height	5'8"
Weight	11-4
Previous club	Dundee United
1998 World Cup qualifiers	4 (Swe, Est - sub, Aus - sub, Lat - sub)

SCOTLAND

DAVID HOPKIN

VITAL STATISTICS

Born	21.8.70. Greenock
Height	5'9"
Weight	10-3
Previous clubs	Morton, Chelsea, Crystal Palace
1998 World Cup qualifiers	2 (Bel, Bel - sub)
Goals	2 (Bel 2 - sub)

DAVID HOPKIN
LEEDS UNITED

Many managers, invited to compile an identikit of their ideal midfield player, would probably come up with someone like Hopkin. George Graham, who demands much, was delighted to buy him from Crystal Palace last summer for £3.25 million.

Hopkin is a match shaper, with his passing, tackling and energy, but he is also a match-winner. He scored 17 goals for Palace last season - including a very late winner from 25 yards against Sheffield United in their play-off at Wembley which lifted Palace back into the Premiership. Chelsea, curiously, didn't rate him very highly. He played only 40 league games for them in three years before they let him go to Palace in 1995 for £800,000.

PROFILES – COUNTRY BY COUNTRY
SCOTLAND

47

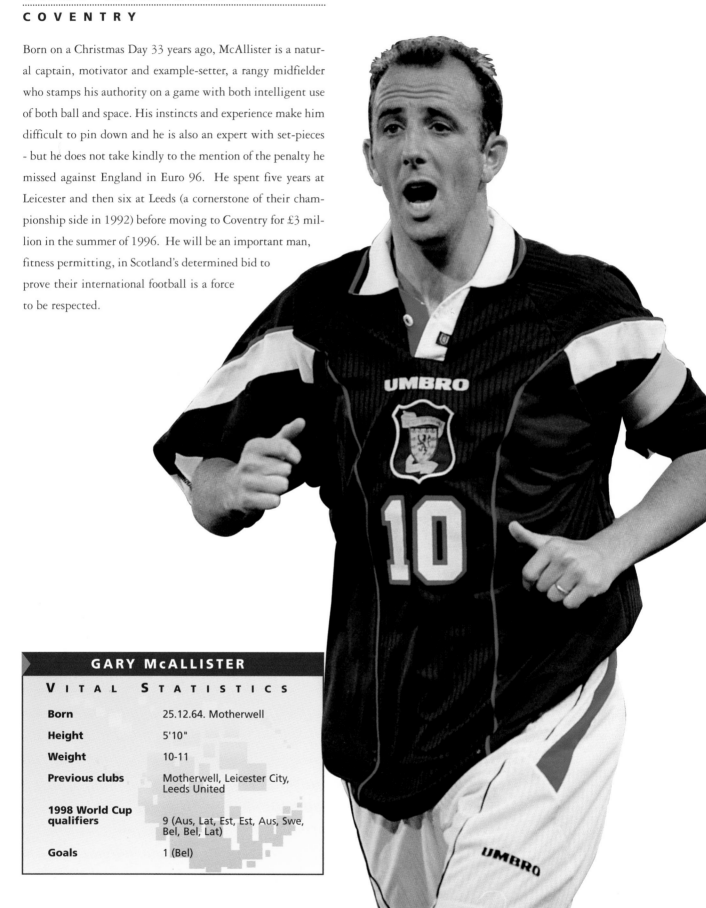

GARY McALLISTER
COVENTRY

Born on a Christmas Day 33 years ago, McAllister is a natural captain, motivator and example-setter, a rangy midfielder who stamps his authority on a game with both intelligent use of both ball and space. His instincts and experience make him difficult to pin down and he is also an expert with set-pieces - but he does not take kindly to the mention of the penalty he missed against England in Euro 96. He spent five years at Leicester and then six at Leeds (a cornerstone of their championship side in 1992) before moving to Coventry for £3 million in the summer of 1996. He will be an important man, fitness permitting, in Scotland's determined bid to prove their international football is a force to be respected.

GARY McALLISTER

VITAL STATISTICS

Born	25.12.64. Motherwell
Height	5'10"
Weight	10-11
Previous clubs	Motherwell, Leicester City, Leeds United
1998 World Cup qualifiers	9 (Aus, Lat, Est, Est, Aus, Swe, Bel, Bel, Lat)
Goals	1 (Bel)

COLIN HENDRY
BLACKBURN ROVERS

One of the best centre-backs in Britain, a Highland rock and a major presence in every game he plays. Earlier in his career he had a reputation as a defensive Jack-the-Lad but now, in his second spell at Ewood Park, he is renowned for his consistency, passion and sheer bloody-mindedness. Hendry's blond hair means he is always very visible, whether dominating, spring-healed, in the air or telescoping a long leg to make a tackle or interception. He guards Blackburn's and Scotland's last ditch with his life but also scores some important goals.

COLIN HENDRY	
V I T A L S T A T I S T I C S	
Born	7.12.65. Keith
Height	6'1"
Weight	12-7
Previous clubs	Dundee, Blackburn Rovers, Manchester City
1998 World Cup qualifiers	7 (Aus, Swe, Est, Est, Aus, Swe, Lat)

KEVIN GALLACHER
BLACKBURN ROVERS

It must be in the blood. His grandfather was Patsy Gallacher, Celtic's 'Mighty Atom' of the 1920s who one or two sane old judges have described as the most brilliant and entertaining player of all time - bar none. Kevin has never quite attracted praise of this kind; but he is certainly an unorthodox front-man of admirable enterprise and great energy. He is a quick thinker and quick mover who likes to run at defences and is always difficult to track or smother. He was a product of the Dundee United youth scheme and found his way to Blackburn, by way of Coventry, for a fee of £1.9 million in 1993. He scored six goals in Scotland's World Cup qualifying games - and Craig Brown, Scotland's manager, says : "Kevin's pace hurts defenders".

KEVIN GALLACHER	
V I T A L S T A T I S T I C S	
Born	23.11.66. Clydebank
Height	5'8"
Weight	11-3
Previous clubs	Dundee United, Coventry City
1998 World Cup qualifiers	8 (Swe - sub, Est, Est, Aus, Swe, Bel, Bel, Lat)

DUNCAN FERGUSON

EVERTON

Every defender's nightmare, a big and combustible gladiator who can look as if he hates everybody and everything, including the ball. Relishes a battle in the air, but is equally prepared to intimidate defenders on the ground - and does so with mean skill. He can sell cheeky dummies, hold up play, deliver measured passes to his wing-men and score from unexpected ranges or even with bicycle-kicks. Ferguson has been with Everton nearly four seasons, after joining them from Rangers for £4.4 million, and he has since had some much publicised brushes with the Law and the Scottish FA. He figured in some of Scotland's qualifying games but has since said that he doesn't want to be considered again. Opposition defenders will be grateful if he doesn't change his mind.

DUNCAN FERGUSON	
V I T A L S T A T I S T I C S	
Born	27.12.71. Stirling
Height	6'4"
Weight	14-6
Previous clubs	Dundee United, Rangers
1998 World Cup qualifiers	2 (Aus, Est)

BELGIUM

The Belgians have been this way many times before - France 98 will be their tenth finals - but still the Red Devils seek that first World Cup Final. Honest Joe, not noted for his generosity, rates them at 50-1.

This is Belgium's fifth consecutive finals appearance and each time they have advanced from the three first-round games. Their temperature rose a few degrees in 1986, when they beat both USSR and Spain in extra time, only to lose in the semi-finals to two Maradona goals to the ultimate champions, Argentina. Alas, there was no consolation third prize as France beat them 4-2 - yet again after extra time.

But hope springs eternal for the nearly men and their new coach Georges Leekons, although the ancients of his team out-number the moderns. Scifo and Van der Elst, up for their fourth finals, will recall their 1994 first-round triumph over neighbours and deadly rivals Holland by a single goal scored by Phillippe Albert. They meet again in Paris on June 13.

PHILLIPPE ALBERT
NEWCASTLE UNITED

Albert is more than a head-banging, ball-wellying stopper. He is tall, easy moving, comfortable in possession and clearly happiest when he has a license to create as well as destroy, a privilege he has not always been allowed at Newcastle. Albert, nonetheless, exudes confidence, a resolute defender but also a man who also excites crowds when he sets off on one of his gallops. He has scored some pretty goals and his long chip over Peter Schmeichel, Manchester United's goal-keeper, three years ago is still talked about with reverence on Tyneside. He joined Newcastle nearly four years ago from Anderlecht for £2.65 million. He indicated - before Belgium qualified! - that his international days were over.

PHILLIPPE ALBERT	
VITAL STATISTICS	
Born	10.8.67. Bouillon
Height	6'3"
Weight	13-0
Previous clubs	Charleroi (Belgium), Mechelen (Belgium), Anderlecht (Belgium)
1998 World Cup qualifiers	3 (Hol, NI, Hol)

CROATIA

Sprung from the Balkans turmoil of the early Nineties, Croatia in their first World Cup year are serious contenders for the big prize. They have a squad of richly-talented and ambitious internationalists, an ABC line-up starting with formidable names in Asanovic, Bilic, Boban and Boksic.

Croatia joined FIFA in 1992 and were soon to announce their presence by reaching the quarter finals of the European Championship, losing to Germany only after eliminating Italy 2-1. They will feel confident of progressing with Argentina to the second round, with a clash with England possibly on the cards, at the expense of Japan and Jamaica.

They qualified the hard way for France, second in their group to Denmark and then battling to a 3-3 victory on aggregate over Ukraine in the play-offs. Afterwards, their coach Miroslav Blazevic acclaimed: "We fought like knights and we are on our way to where we belong, where we will prove that we are a football nation."

Confidence rating: Ten out of ten!

SLAVEN BILIC
EVERTON

Bilic is a central pillar of Croatia's defence and has made his mark on the English game with accomplished ease - first with West Ham, becoming one of the Upton Park crowd's favourite players, and now with Everton. The Merseyside club paid £4.5 million for him, then a British record for a defender, just after the close of last season.

Bilic is a player of obvious class, resolute, consistent and able to make room or time for himself in the tightest situations. He is a big and intelligent man, a linguist with a mind of his own, and this is reflected in his constructive play. He has occasional disciplinary hiccups, but he is a durable character who doesn't miss many games or make many mistakes.

SLAVEN BILIC	
VITAL STATISTICS	
Born	11.9.98. Split
Height	6'2"
Weight	13-2
Previous clubs	Hadjuk Split (Croatia), Karlsruhe (Germany),West Ham United
1998 World Cup qualifiers	9 (Bos, Gre, Den, Slo, Gre, Bos, Den, Slo,Ukr)
Goals	3 (Bos, Bos, Uhr)

DENMARK

*N*othing is impossible when you have probably the best goalkeeper in the world. That was the opinion of every red-blooded Dane as Peter Schmeichel brought off a fantastic save against Greece to keep it at 0-0 in the final, decisive group match. That point consigned Croatia to two bitter play-off games with Ukraine. Denmark had been shocked by a 3-0 defeat against Bosnia, their only qualifying-round upset, but they showed steel and resolution in taking four points from the clashes with Croatia and Greece.

The Danes emerged as serious international competitors when they won through to the 1986 World Cup finals for the first time. They beat all three group opponents - Scotland 1-0, Uruguay 6-1, West Germany 2-0 - before losing in the second round 5-1 to Spain, Emilio Butragueno scoring four.

Since then, Denmark have grown in stature. In the 1990 qualifiers, they missed out to Romania by one point; in the 1994 series, they failed to qualify by a whisker on level points with Eire. And in 1992, they were surprising winners of the European Championship, having become involved only as late-hour replacements for the expelled Yugoslavia.

JON DAHL TOMASSON
NEWCASTLE UNITED

Tomasson was pursued and wooed by a host of big European clubs, including Barcelona, but chose to join Newcastle who paid Heerenveen £2.2 million for him last summer. Tomasson, now 21, is something of a hero in Denmark, despite playing in Holland since he was 17, but the number and quality of the goals he scored meant a move to bigger things was inevitable. He can play in midfield or as a striker, though the position he prefers is just behind the main spearhead. His speed takes him into critical areas and his timing and positive attitude means he is regularly on the end of half-chances. He played his first game for Denmark against Croatia, a World Cup qualifier, in March 1997.

JON DAHL TOMASSON	
V I T A L S T A T I S T I C S	
Born	29.8.76. Copenhagen
Height	6'0"
Weight	11-0
Previous club	Koge BK (Denmark), Heerenveen (Holland)
1998 World Cup qualifiers	4 (Cro - sub, Slo, Bos, Bos)

ALLAN NIELSEN
TOTTENHAM HOTSPUR

Nielsen is an action man with a good track record at both club and international level, a tenacious box-to-box midfielder who joined Spurs from Brondby at the start of the 1996-97 season. His experience has been varied: he went to Bayern Munich at the age of 17 - and Brondby, one of several Danish clubs he played for later on, were Danish champions and conquerors of Liverpool in the UEFA Cup in 1995-96. Nielsen scored within a minute of his international debut as a second-half substitute against Armenia in 1995, and has figured in Denmark's plans ever since.

ALAN NIELSEN

VITAL STATISTICS

Born	13.3.71. Esbjerg
Height	5'8"
Weight	11-2
Previous clubs	Bayern Munich (Switzerland), Sion (Switzerland), Odense (Denmark), FC Copenhagen (Denmark), Brondby (Demark)
1998 World Cup qualifiers	8 (Slo, Gre Cro, SLo, Bos, Bos, Cro, Gre)
Goals	3 (Slo, Slo 2)

CLAUS THOMSEN
EVERTON

Thomsen is a tall and competitive defender who has had mixed fortunes with Everton; but, then, Everton have been a mixed up lot themselves. He moved from Aarhus to Ipswich in 1994 and then onto Everton early in 1997. He was a Goodison regular to begin with, mainly in midfield, but his first team appearances have since been limited. Solid in the air and tackles and passes with care and accuracy.

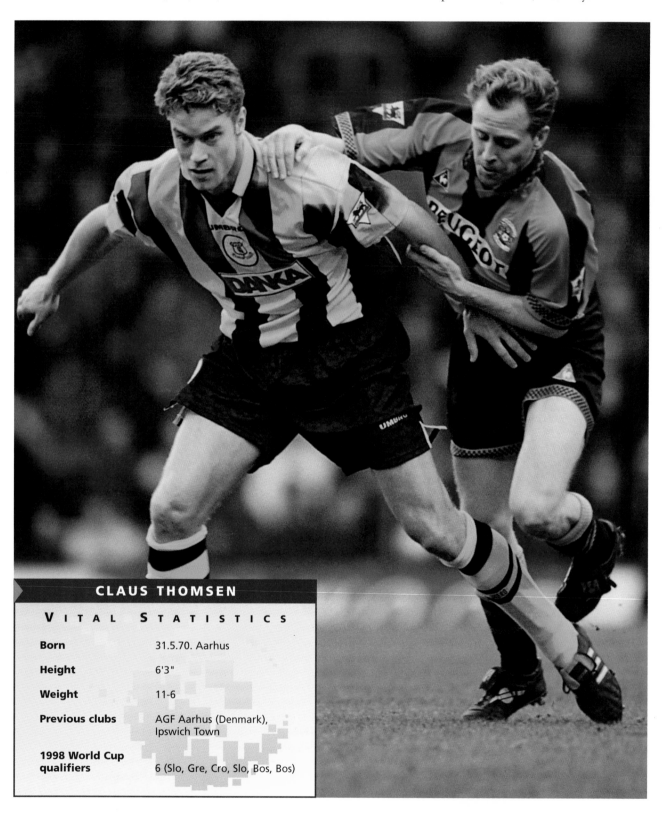

CLAUS THOMSEN

VITAL STATISTICS

Born	31.5.70. Aarhus
Height	6'3"
Weight	11-6
Previous clubs	AGF Aarhus (Denmark), Ipswich Town
1998 World Cup qualifiers	6 (Slo, Gre, Cro, Slo, Bos, Bos)

JACOB LAURSEN
DERBY COUNTY

The Danes have always been natural travellers - and Laursen is no exception. He moved from Silkeborg, winner of the Danish championship in 1994, to Derby nearly two years ago and immediately acclimatized himself to the rigours of the Premiership. He has been instrumental in Derby's establishment as a top-rank side again, playing anywhere in defence with the awareness of someone who has also operated in midfield. He does things simply and well - no fuss, no histrionics - and reads the game intelligently. He was a member of Denmark's squad in Euro 96.

JACOB LAURSEN

VITAL STATISTICS

Born	6.10.71. Vejle
Height	5'11"
Weight	12-1
Previous clubs	Vejle (Denmark), Silkeborg (Denmark)
1998 World Cup qualifiers	6 (Slo, Gre, Cro, Slo, Bos, Bos)

PETER SCHMEICHEL
MANCHESTER UNITED

Schmeichel is a goalkeeper any country in the world would be grateful to have, a blond giant who has known only success in the Nineties. He is 6ft 4 ins tall, 15 stone plus, aggressive and very noisy - never conceding that any goal is remotely his fault. He dominates his area, is bullishly confident in the air and is a wonderful shot-stopper. He spreads himself enormously and usually, somehow, manages to get part of his anatomy in the way of the ball. He also has a long and lancing throw, a legacy of his early handball days in Denmark, which turns defence into attack in a twinkling. Joined Manchester United from Brondby for £550,000 in 1991, played a major role in Denmark's European championship triumph a year later and, since then, has been a key-man in the old Trafford success story.

PETER SCHMEICHEL	
VITAL STATISTICS	
Born	18.11.63. Gladsaxe
Height	6'4"
Weight	15-13
Previous clubs	Hvidore (Denmark) Brondby (Denmark)
1998 World Cup qualifiers	8 (Slo, Gre, Cro, Slo, Bos, Bos, Cro, Gre)

PER FRANDSEN
BOLTON WANDERERS

A stormtrooper in midfield who has occasional differences of opinion with referees; but Frandsen's attitude is good and he is an unselfish team-man who keeps to a game-plan. His technique is impressive and he is always a threat when pushing forward. His shot is powerful and he is a crafty poacher. Frandsen was a Cup-winner in Denmark and had experience in France before joining Bolton in the summer of 1996 - a shrewd acquisition because he became a key figure, missing only a handful of games, in the Lancashire club's promotion push to the Premiership. Bolton's fans have much respect for him.

PER FRANDSEN
VITAL STATISTICS

Born	6.2.70. Copenhagen
Height	6'1"
Weight	12-6
Previous clubs	B1903 Copenhagen, Lille, FC Copenhagen
1998 World Cup qualifiers	4 (Cro, Slo - sub, Bos - sub, Cro)

FRANCE

France have the considerable advantage of all home matches as they enter their tenth World Cup finals. That alone should justify their high place in the betting stakes. Five of the 15 Finals have been won by the host nation.

The French are the 'nearly men' of the competition, with three semi-final defeats to their debit, two third places to their credit. Just Fontaine set up a scoring record with 13 in 1958, but Pele's hat-trick inspired Brazil to a 5-2 victory over the French. West Germany were their semi-final conquerors in 1982, by 5-4 on penalties following a 3-3 extra-time score line. Four years on and the Germans were again the villains, this time by 2-0 in Mexico.

That West German double in the semi-finals was cruel vengeance for the third-place play-off of 1958, when four goals by Fontaine helped France to a spectacular 6-3 triumph.

Their coach Aime Jacquet aims to say his Parisian farewells with a final Final celebration at the magnificent new Stade de France. Bonne chance, Aime!

PATRICK VIEIRA
ARSENAL

Arsenal bought Vieira from AC Milan on the say-so of Arsene Wenger before he became manager at Highbury. Vieira was under-employed by the Italian club, his career needed re-launching and so, for a comparatively modest £3.5 million, Arsenal acquired a player who bristles with quality. Vieira is tall, stylish, highly committed (too much so in the opinion of some referees) and adjusts easily. He tackles weightily and is comfortable in possession, a difficult man to knock off the ball. His technique is polished and his passing can be inspired - a superior act in midfield and a player who likes to take command. Vieira concedes there will be pressure on France because they are hosts but says "if we are on top of our game we have a chance".

PATRICK VIEIRA	
VITAL STATISTICS	
Born	23.6.76. Dakar (Senegal)
Height	6'4"
Weight	13-0
Previous clubs	Cannes (France), AC Milan (Italy)

FRANK LEBOEUF
CHELSEA

A very model of a modern defender: tall, lean, composed and never prepared to confine himself to the drudgery of guard duty. A centre-half or sweeper who is prepared to mix it with the best - but also an adventurer who distributed accurately and has scored some handsome goals. He can hit a dead ball as hard as anyone in the game, yet often coverts penalties with casual ease. Leboeuf is a regular member of the French squad and says playing in England has made him brighter both

mentally and physically. The draw for the World Cup finals took place in his home-town Marseille - "since when" he says "the World Cup has gripped the whole of France".

FRANK LEBOEUF

VITAL STATISTICS

Born	22.1.68. Paris
Height	6'0"
Weight	12-0
Previous clubs	Laval (France), Strasbourg (France)

EMMANUEL PETIT
ARSENAL

A distinctive figure with his pony-tail, a stylist off and on the field. He spent nine years with Monaco before joining Arsenal a season ago and, at 27, he says he is still learning the game and that his best is still to come. He used to be a defender but now plays in midfield which allows him more expression with his educated left foot and bright perception. Arsenal weren't the only club to recognise his ability: Tottenham. Real Madrid and Inter Milan were among other clubs which courted him - but the influence of Arsene Wenger, once of Monaco, now of Highbury, was decisive. Pele and George Best, two fair judges, have praised his talent.

EMMANUEL PETIT	
VITAL STATISTICS	
Born	22.9.70. Dieppe
Height	6'2"
Weight	12-9
Previous clubs	Monaco (France)

GERMANY

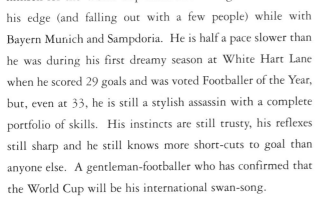

*W*est Germany, and now unified Germany, have had the luck of the draw and are seeded to meet Brazil in the 1998 Final, with the score 4-3 to the South Americans in the winner's table. Their form in the qualifiers was not so hot, for though they were unbeaten with six wins and four draws, they had a daunting last match at home to Albania. With the score at 3-3, Oliver Bierhoff scored the winner in the last minute.

The Germans have never failed in their qualifying rounds; they have contested six of the last 11 Finals; they have twice won third place. They will take on USA in their first match with the nucleus of their side drawn from Borussia Dortmund, the European champions of 1997 and conquerors of Manchester United. Their star performer from Dortmund is Matthias Sammer, sweeper supreme and 1997 European Footballer of the year.

The Germans have never met two of their group, Iran and USA, in the World Cup, but they will face rugged old rivals in Yugoslavia. They have clashed five times in finals, four of them remarkably in quarter-final matches. The score to date: West Germany 4 Yugoslavia 1.

JURGEN KLINSMANN

TOTTENHAM HOTSPUR

Klinsmann came and conquered...and went...and now he is back again. Germany's captain returned to the Premiership just before Christmas to do a job for Tottenham and, equally, to fine tune himself for the World Cup finals after losing his edge (and falling out with a few people) while with Bayern Munich and Sampdoria. He is half a pace slower than he was during his first dreamy season at White Hart Lane when he scored 29 goals and was voted Footballer of the Year, but, even at 33, he is still a stylish assassin with a complete portfolio of skills. His instincts are still trusty, his reflexes still sharp and he still knows more short-cuts to goal than anyone else. A gentleman-footballer who has confirmed that the World Cup will be his international swan-song.

JURGEN KLINSMANN	
VITAL STATISTICS	
Born	30.7.64. Goppingen
Height	6'2"
Weight	12-2
Previous clubs	Stuttgart Kickers (Germany), VfB Stuttgart (Germany), Inter Milan (Italy), Monaco (France), Tottenham (England), Bayern Munich (Germany),Sampdoria (Italy)
1998 World Cup qualifiers	9 (Arm, NIre, Por, Alb, Ukr, Ukr, NIre, Por, Arm)
World Cup final games	12 (1990 Yug, UAE, Col, Hol, Cze, Eng, Arg; 1994 Bol, Spa, SKor, Bel, Bul)
Goals	8 (1990 Yug, UAE, Hol; 1994 Bol, Spa, SKor 2, Bel)
Honours	1990 World Cup winners medal

HOLLAND

The clever money has gone on Holland at 8-1, as they say in betting circles. Certainly, theirs is not the most testing group with Belgium, South Korea and Mexico as opponents. The Dutch are looking to win through the first round for their third consecutive time in the finals.

The one concern is their unpredictability. They won splendidly twice against Belgium in the 1998 qualifiers with a 6-1 aggregate; unaccountably, they shed five out of six points against Turkey. Then again, they demolished Wales 10-2 in two meetings.

Holland's World Cup history is as jerky as a jumping-jack. Twice in the pre-War finals, they were beaten by the Swiss then the Czechs. Twice in the Seventies, they charmed the world with their Total Football; twice sadly they were engulfed by the power play of their Final opponents, West Germany (1974) and Argentina (1978). Twice in the Nineties, they put on the Dutch charm and both times were eliminated, narrowly, by the ultimate champions, West Germany (1-2 in 1990) and Brazil (2-3 in 1994).

Now it is up to Bergkamp, Overmars and Kluivert to redress the issue. The clever money suggests they'll be third time lucky.

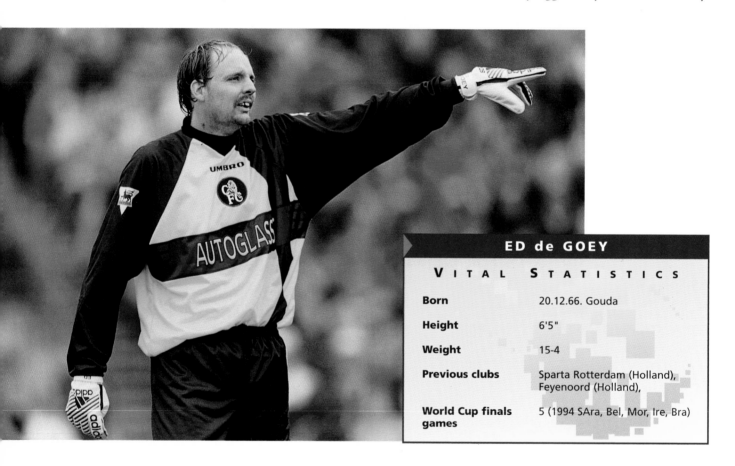

ED de GOEY	
V I T A L	**S T A T I S T I C S**
Born	20.12.66. Gouda
Height	6'5"
Weight	15-4
Previous clubs	Sparta Rotterdam (Holland), Feyenoord (Holland),
World Cup finals games	5 (1994 SAra, Bel, Mor, Ire, Bra)

ED de GOEY
CHELSEA

A monument of a goalkeeper, de Goey jumped at the chance of working with Ruud Gullit at Chelsea. He joined them from Feyenoord for £2 million or so last summer. De Goey can be a difficult man to beat and among his top moments this season were two saves he made during Chelsea's penalty shoot-out with Ipswich in the quarter-finals of the Coca Cola Cup. Dennis Wise commented: "Big Ed...he's large enough to frighten the life out of you". De Goey figured prominently in the 1994 World Cup finals when Holland reached the quarter-finals - beaten in the end by 3-2 by the eventual champions Brazil.

DENNIS BERGKAMP
ARSENAL

Bergkamp has been described as one of the best players in the world so often that there must be something in it. Bergkamp, himself, is a modest man who seems to find such praise embarrassing. His early days with Johan Cruyff at Ajax, the corrosive pressure of Italian football with Inter Milan and his three high-profile years in north London have provided him with a treasury of experience and an ability to keep things in perspective. His value to Arsenal and Holland, however, is enormous. He sets toweringly high standards for himself, works hard at his game (especially on what he regards as his weaknesses) and pays great attention to detail. He is a high-tec and creative striker, ice-cool in the heat of battle, won't be bullied and is very much a team-man. He can score from any range and angle and, though he doesn't score with every shot, he is usually on target. And he can make the difficult look ludicrously easy.

DENNIS BERGKAMP	
V I T A L S T A T I S T I C S	
Born	18.5.69. Amsterdam
Height	6'0"
Weight	12-5
1998 World Cup qualifiers	6 (Wal, Bel, SMar, SMar, Bel, Tur)
Goals	7 (Wal 3, Bel, Mor, Ire, Bra)
World Cup finals games	5 (SAra, Bel, Mor, Ire, Bra)
Goals	3 (Mor, Ire, Bra)

MARC OVERMARS

ARSENAL

Overmars has a cabinet of silver to prove he can play football better than most: 1995 World championship winner, 1995 European Cup, three Dutch championships, Dutch Cup etc, etc - and he still regrets missing the European championship

and European Cup final in 1996 because of ligament trouble. Arsenal paid Ajax £7 million for him last summer and, after a cautious start, he has been showing the form which convinced many people he is one of the best wingers in Europe. He is a trim and finely balanced player with sharp variations in pace and direction, a mazy dribbler who crosses intelligently and has a stinging finish. He is sometimes accused of holding the ball too long but, then, he is also accused sometimes of releasing it too quickly. And as Dennis Bergkamp says: "It's sometimes overlooked that Marc attracts a lot of attention from defenders and this makes space for others in his team".

MARC OVERMARS	
VITAL STATISTICS	
Born	29.3.73. Emst
Height	5'9"
Weight	11-10
Previous clubs	Go Ahead Eagles (Holland), Willem II Tilburg (Holland), Ajax (Holland)
1998 World Cup qualifiers	5 (Wal, Bel, SMar, Tur, Tur – all as sub)
World Cup finals games	5 (SAra, Bel - sub, Mor Ire, Bra)

ITALY

Italy have seen it all and done it all - and they're here again by the skin of their teeth. That's the way it has invariably been for them in the World Cup - the last-gasp survivors of early matches leading up to a grand finale. Now for France and more brinkmanship par excellence?

Italy have played in the Final five times, winning three. They will be in their 14th finals along with Germany and two fewer than ever-present Brazil. They missed out only in 1958, being eliminated astonishingly by Northern Ireland under their wily manager Peter Doherty and skipper Danny Blanchflower.

Their group opponents in 1998 are Chile, Cameroon and Austria. Past meetings points to a safe passage. Indeed, their only clash with Cameroon, a 1-1 draw, led to Final victory in 1982 over West Germany. They met Chile in 1962 and 1966 - lost 2-0, won 2-0. Three times they have faced Austria, winning 1-0 every time.

Perhaps a new page in World Cup history is about to be written by Italy. The Father-and-Son Final, starring coach Cesare Maldini and captain Paolo Maldini.

ROBERTO DI MATTEO

CHELSEA

"We have great confidence in ourselves...we believe we are going to do very well" says Di Matteo of Italy's prospects in France. Di Matteo believes in himself as well: it is one of the keys to his authority in midfield. Di Matteo is an inventive co-ordinator who reads the game well. He has a good engine, a slick change of gear and an eye for the main chance. His long, dipping opener after just 43 seconds of the 1997 FA Cup final was one of Wembley's best. He is also a perfectionist, from the way he dresses and patiently signs autographs to his training and thinking about the game.

Di Matteo was raised in Switzerland by Italian parents and has learnt to speak fluent English since joining Chelsea from Lazio for £4.9 million in the summer of 1996.

ROBERTO DI MATTEO	
VITAL STATISTICS	
Born	29.5. 70. Sciaffusa
Height	5'10"
Weight	12-0
Previous clubs	Schaffhausen (Switzerland), FC Zurich (Switzerland), FC Aarau (Switzerland), Lazio (Italy)
1998 World Cup qualifiers	9 (Mol, Geo, Eng, Mol, Pol, Pol, Geo, Rus, Rus)

GIANFRANCO ZOLA
CHELSEA

The style and the smile say it all. Zola rounded off his first season in Chelsea blue with an FA Cup winner's medal and the Footballer of the Year trophy. One of English football's most popular imports - even though he did score Italy's winner against England at Wembley. "Just doing my job" he says.

The little Sardinian is a master-footballer, subtle, creative, elusive, impudent, quick-thinking, lethal from any angle and height with his shooting and, as England discovered, able to turn a match with a moment of inspiration. He joined Chelsea from Parma for £4.5 million in November 1996 and, even in a team creaking with stars, he soon became a cult figure. "France will probably be my last tournament for Italy" he says "and I am very, very focussed on it."

GIANFRANCO ZOLA

V I T A L   S T A T I S T I C S

Born	7.7.66. Oliena
Height	5'5"
Weight	10-2
Previous clubs	Napoli (Italy), Parma (Italy)
1998 World Cup qualifiers	8 (Mol, Geo, Eng, Mol, Pol, Pol, Geo, Eng)
Goals	2 (Eng, Mol)
World Cup finals games	1 (1994 Bul (sub) - sent off)

ATTILIO LOMBARDO
CRYSTAL PALACE

An outstanding buy for Crystal Palace - just £1.6 million from Juventus last August after much talk about the small-print in his contract. Lombardo is an attacking midfielder with everything...except hair on his head and an ability to avoid injuries. He even pulled a thigh muscle while back-heeling a ball during Italy's preparation for one of their World Cup play-off matches against Russia. His experience gives point to a full quiver of skills which includes a sensitive touch and a dramatic change of pace.

ATTILIO LOMBARDO	
VITAL STATISTICS	
Born	6.1.66. Zelo Buon
Height	5'9"
Weight	11-8
Previous clubs	Cremonese (Italy), Sampdoria (Italy), Juventus (Italy)
1998 World Cup qualifiers	1 (Geo)

JAMAICA

Jamaica's way to the stars began on March 31, 1996 - Surinam 0 Jamaica 1 - and finally took off 19 qualifying matches later on November 16, 1996 - Jamaica 1 Mexico 0. Now they are in the finals at their sixth attempt, having settled old scores against Costa Rica, El Salvador and Canada.

The flight of the Reggae Boyz began with the arrival of their coach Rene Simoes from Brazil. He has become a cult figure in the Caribbean, where even Test cricket has taken second place to football with the sporting public. He has bonded a collection of local lads and English-based players into a squad brimming with confidence and not a little skill.

"Simoes is a brilliant coach," says Fitzroy Simpson, one of the 'English' Boyz. "He is to Jamaica what Jack Charlton was to Ireland." When they drew 0-0 with Mexico to qualify for France, a national holiday was declared. What will happen if Jamaica beat Croatia in Lens on June 14 is impossible to imagine!

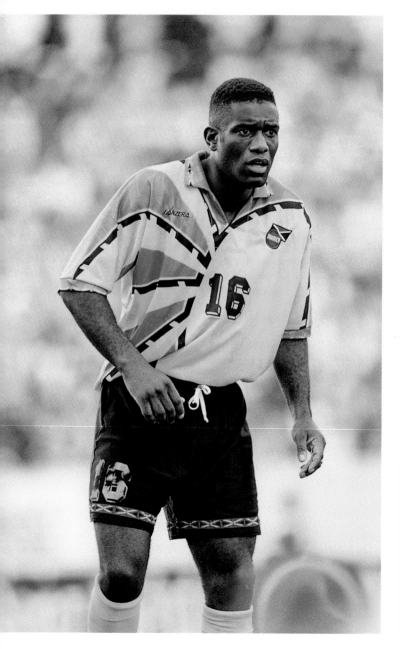

ROBBIE EARLE
WIMBLEDON

Earle would like to have played for England but the nearest he got was one "stand-by" invitation. He chose, instead, to represent his parents' homeland and found himself on a magic carpet - part of Jamaica's World Cup odyssey. His role as an attacking and scoring midfielder will be a key one but as a Wimbledon man, a member of the Crazy Gang, he knows what it takes to upset the odds. He is persuasively strong, disarmingly direct and a perpetual threat anywhere near the opposition's net. The number of goals he scores compares well with any midfielder in the Premiership. "Jamaica are better technically than they're given credit for" he says. "We have a point to prove in France" - and his hazy dream is that Jamaica and England will somehow come face to face.

ROBBIE EARLE	
VITAL STATISTICS	
Born	27.1.65. Newcastle under Lyme
Height	5'9"
Previous club	Port Vale
1998 World Cup qualifiers	4 (Can, CRic - sub, USA - sub, Mex - sub)

DEON BURTON
DERBY COUNTY

A year ago Burton was struggling to make Portsmouth's side in the Nationwide First Division. Now he is a Premiership man with Derby and looking forward to the World Cup finals as one of the Reggae Boyz of Jamaica - and a carnival is guaranteed. "Fairytale?" he says. "The word is inadequate".

Burton, open-faced and a real smiler, was born in England but his father came from Jamaica. He followed manager Jim Smith from Portsmouth to Derby and, his confidence growing, he scored in four consecutive internationals, including the winners against Costa Rica and Canada. He is a highly mobile striker, smells opportunity and accepts responsibility.

The Reggae Boyz enjoy themselves but they also take their football very seriously. They do their homework, train hard, respond to big-time atmosphere - and play an organised game with a few flash touches.

DEON BURTON	
VITAL STATISTICS	
Born	25.10.76. Ashford
Height	5'8"
Weight	10-9
Previous clubs	Portsmouth, Cardiff City (loan)
1998 World Cup qualifiers	5 (Can, CRic, USA, Sal, Mex)
Goals	4 (Can, CRic, USA, Sal)

MARCUS GAYLE
WIMBLEDON

Gayle's father is from Jamaica, his mother from Barbados and he learnt his early football on Shepherd's Bush Green in West London before playing for England's Youth team. But there were no further calls from Lancaster Gate and now he plans to make his mark on the international scene with Jamaica. He joined Wimbledon from Brentford for £250,000 in 1994 and has proved one of their best investments, a striker or mid-fielder who is laid back off the field but always in top gear on it. Gayle is aggressive and confident, runs hard and straight, can beat a man, flicks the ball about cleverly and is always a danger in front of goal. He is very positive with his head and his left foot gives him a chance from any range. Wimbledon claimed Gayle was ineligible to play for Jamaica; but FIFA, the game's governing body, gave him clearance.

MARCUS GAYLE
VITAL STATISTICS

Born	27.9.70. Hammersmith
Height	6'1"
Weight	12-9
Previous club	Brentford

NIGERIA

*O*ut of Africa and clearly the spearhead of a five-nation challenge, Nigeria will lack nothing for confidence. On their finals debut at USA '94, they headed their group and then gave Italy a nerve-shattering experience in the second round.

The Africans led from an Emmanuel Amunike goal until two minutes from the 90- minute whistle, when Roberto Baggio equalised. Italy scored again in extra time, Roberto this time from the penalty spot, and the Latin sighs of relief echoed all the way to the final with Brazil.

Nigeria's power and potential was there for all to see, and any lingering doubts were dispelled two years later when they became Olympic champions. Ekoku (Wimbledon) and Babayaro (Chelsea) will tell of the best yet to come from the likes of Victor Ikpeba of Monaco - the African Player of the Year - and from Tijani Babangida of Ajax, Daniel Amokachi and the incredible Nwankwo Kanu of Inter Milan.

Kanu is quite literally the heartbeat of Nigerian fans. In the summer of 1996, he underwent major surgery on a faulty heart valve and didn't play again for a year. Now he is back and playing alongside Ronaldo.

Nigeria have surely taken over from Cameroon as the lions of Africa.

CELESTINE BABAYARO
CHELSEA

Everything is happening so fast for Babayaro that it is a wonder his feet are still on the ground - though that's the last place they are whenever he scores. A celebratory somersault, high and flamboyant, is one of his trademarks. Babayaro joined Chelsea for £2.25 million in the summer of 1997 after winning a hold-all full of gongs and awards with Anderlecht and Nigeria, including a Belgian championship and Olympic gold during the Atlanta Games in 1996 ("The greatest achievement of my career").

The 19-year-old wing back's talent and promise were so obvious that a string of clubs, including Inter-Milan and Juventus, tried to buy him. But the style and rewards of English football, the cosmopolitan appeal of Chelsea and his respect for Ruud Gullit lured him to London. Babayaro is quick, aggressive and two-footed, a resolute defender but also a natural raider. "Everyone now realises Africa is a powerful force in football" he says "which means we no longer have surprise on our side".

CELESTINE BABAYARO

VITAL STATISTICS

Born	29.8.78. Kadun
Height	5'7"
Weight	10-10
Previous club	Anderlecht (Belgium)
1998 World Cup qualifiers	4 (Ken, Gui, Buk, Ken)

EFAN EKOKU
WIMBLEDON

Not even Wimbledon always get it right when it comes to netting young talent. Wimbledon paid a club record £900,000 for Ekoku in 1994 - a big bill for someone who had unsuccessfully applied for a trial with them before making his name with Sutton United, Bournemouth and Norwich. Efan (short for Efangwu) is a versatile front man who is lightning quick, strong and an incisive finisher who seems to get busier as a game gets older. His father is a high-ranker in Nigeria and Efan, a man with a wry sense of humour, is known by Wimbledon's Crazy Gang as 'The Chief'.

EFAN EKOKU
VITAL STATISTICS

Born	8.6.67. Manchester
Height	6'1"
Weight	12-0
Previous clubs	Bournemouth, Norwich City

Norway's standing in European football has grown enormously since commentator Borge Lillelien's passionate eulogy after their first victory against England in Oslo in 1981. "We are the best in the world" he roared. "We have beaten England. Lord Nelson, Lord Beaverbrook, Sir Winston Churchill, Sir Anthony Eden, Clement Atlee, Henry Cooper, Lady Diana. We have beaten them all. Maggie Thatcher, can you hear me? Maggie Thatcher, your boys took a helluva beating".

More than 30 Norwegians play in English football, over half of them in the Premiership, and they flourish because they are good athletes, committed, disciplined, acclimatize easily and, importantly, have talent. Egil Olsen, Norway's manger, says the experience they are gaining is valuable - but adds that there is also a downside. "Not all Premiership clubs play at the same level, and many of my players are not playing all the time".

FRODE GRODAS
TOTTENHAM HOTSPUR

Agile and stable goalkeeper who joined Chelsea as cover, on a free transfer from Lillestrom in 1996, and impressed enough to be given a contract. He was at his best in Chelsea's F.A. Cup semi-final against Wimbledon last season and was a member of their winning team at Wembley. Enjoys the big occasion and has regular moments of inspiration. Moved to Tottenham in mid season.

FRODE GRODAS

VITAL STATISTICS	
Born	24.10.64. Sogndal
Height	6'2"
Weight	14-7
Previous clubs	Sogndal (Norway), Lillestrom (Norway)
1998 World Cup qualifiers	8 (Azer, Hun, Swi, Fin, Hon, Fin, Azer, Swi)

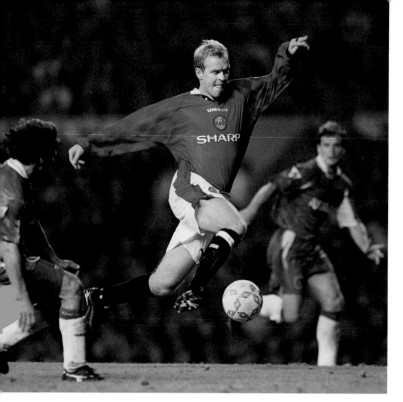

HENNING BERG

HENNING BERG	
V I T A L S T A T I S T I C S	
Born	1.9.68. Eidsvoll
Height	6'0"
Weight	12-4
Previous clubs	Lillestrom (Norway), Blackburn Rovers
1998 World Cup Qualifiers	8 (Azer, Hun, Swi, Fin, Hun, Fin, Azer, Swi)
World Cup finals games	3 (1994 Mex, Ita, Ire)

HENNING BERG
MANCHESTER UNITED

High class member of Blackburn's championship defence in 1995 and now, after his £5 million move to Manchester United last August, is in line for more glory. His reading of the game, positioning and timing can be outstanding and, although he doesn't win every ball in the air, he is much respected by fellow professionals. Twice voted Norway's Footballer of the year.

BJORN-TORE KVARME	
V I T A L S T A T I S T I C S	
Born	17.7.72. Trondheim
Height	6'1"
Weight	12-4
Previous Club	Rosenborg Trondheim (Norway)

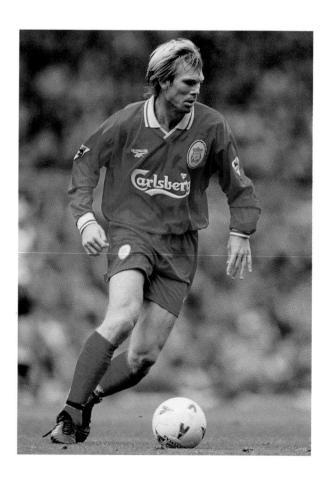

BJORN-TORE KVARME
LIVERPOOL

Combative defender who settled quickly at Anfield after joining Liverpool from Rosenborg, early in 1997, on a free transfer under the Bosman ruling. Wins the ball decisively and uses it astutely. A fighter who hates to lose but has not been able to pin down a regular first-team this season. As a boy, in Norway, he supported Tottenham.

LARS BOHINEN
BLACKBURN ROVERS

A controversial midfielder who can be a match-winner but whose career has been blighted by inconsistent periods. His move from Nottingham Forest to Blackburn in 1995 was an acrimonious affair: a clause in his contract enabled him to move for a modest fee. His control and distribution are clever and he has scored some memorable goals (including a winner against Italy in 1991 and a clincher against England in 1993) but he has also spoken publicly about his lack of international opportunity - which is never recommended.

LARS BOHINEN	
V I T A L S T A T I S T I C S	
Born	8.9.69. Vadso
Height	6'1"
Weight	12-1
Previous clubs	Valerengen (Norway), Viking Stavanger (Norway), Young Boys Berne (Switzerland), Nottingham Forest
1998 World Cup Qualifiers	1 (Hun)
World Cup finals games	3 (1994 Mex, Ita, Ire - sub)

STIG-INGE BJORNEBYE
LIVERPOOL

Richly experienced international who is consistent, irrepressible and a constant headache to opponents along his left touch line. An excellent crosser of the ball, always with his left foot, often driven with great pace, but never neglects his defensive responsibilities. Cost Liverpool a modest £600,000 when they signed him from Rosenborg in 1992.

STIG-INGE BJORNEBYE	
V I T A L S T A T I S T I C S	
Born	11.12.69. Strannen
Height	5'10"
Weight	11-9
Previous clubs	Kongsvinger (Norway), Rosenborg Trondheim (Norway)
1998 World Cup Qualifiers	7 (Azer, Hun, Fin, Hun, Fin, Azer, Swi)
World Cup finals games	3 (1994 Mex, Ita, Ire)

ALF-INGE HAALAND
LEEDS UNITED

Haaland moved from Nottingham Forest to Elland Road for £1.6 million last summer - an influential figure in midfield who is noted for his buccaneering runs and powerful shooting. But, equally, he is also a valuable utility man who can plug any hole in defence. A stern tackler and marker.

ALF-INGE HAALAND	
V I T A L S T A T I S T I C S	
Born	23.11.72. Stavanger
Height	5'10"
Weight	12-12
Previous clubs	Bryne (Norway), Nottingham Forest
1998 World Cup qualifiers	6 (Azer, Hun, Swi, Hun, Fin - sub, Swi - sub)

RONNY JOHNSEN
MANCHESTER UNITED

One of Alex Ferguson's best signings. Johnsen moved from Besiktas (Turkey) for £1.2 million in 1996 and has established himself as a rock at the heart of the champions' defence. A warrior and an innovator, composed, tireless and aware of everything. "Norwegians in England are playing in the world's toughest league" he says. "That must be a plus".

RONNY JOHNSEN	
VITAL STATISTICS	
Born	10.6.69. Sandelfjord
Height	6'3"
Weight	13-1
Previous clubs	Eik (Norway), Lyn Oslo (Norway), Lillestrom (Norway), Besitkas (Turkey)
1998 World Cup qualifiers	5 (Azer, Hun, Swi, Fin, Hun)

EGIL OSTENSTAD
SOUTHAMPTON

Unorthodox striker who has made a big impression in his two seasons at the Dell - especially on the day he contributed a hat-trick to Southampton's 6-3 defeat of Manchester United. Sparkling feet, bright mind, difficult to mark and adept at holding the ball until support arrives. Relishes responsibility and often plays as a lone striker. He supported Liverpool as a boy and wants to become a lawyer.

EGIL OSTENSTAD	
VITAL STATISTICS	
Born	2.1.72. Hagesund
Height	5'11"
Weight	13-0
Previous club	Viking Stavanger (Norway)
1998 World Cup qualifiers	4 (Hun -sub, Swi, Hun - sub, Swi - sub)
Goals	1 (Swi)

TORE-ANDRE FLO
CHELSEA

Flo scored twice against Brazil last year and emphasised his value to Norway with some decisive strikes in their World Cup qualifiers. His height makes him a menace in the air and his experience with Chelsea, since joining them from Brann Bergen fro £300,000 last summer, has widened his range and improved his confidence. He says Norway's group game with Brazil in Marseille will not be their most important - "We must beat Scotland and Morocco to qualify in second place".

TORE-ANDRE FLO	
VITAL STATISTICS	
Born	15.6.73. Sogndal
Height	6'2"
Weight	12-6
Previous clubs	Sogndal (Norway), Tromso (Norway), Brann Bergen (Norway)
1998 World Cup qualifiers	7 (Azer - sub, Swi, Fin, Hun, Fin, Azer, Swi)
Goals	3 (Fin, Azer, Swi)

OYVIND LEONHARDSEN
LIVERPOOL

Talented, determined and much admired attacking midfielder who scored one of the two goals which enabled Norway to beat Graham Taylor's England in a World Cup qualifier in 1993. Wimbledon, those wheeler-dealers, bought him for £660,000 in 1994 and sold him to Liverpool for £3.5 million last summer - an honest price, nonetheless, for a player who can unlock the tightest of defences.

OYVIND LEONHARDSEN	
VITAL STATISTICS	
Born	17.8.70. Molde
Height	5'10"
Weight	11-2
Previous clubs	Molde (Norway), Rosenborg Trondheim (Norway), Wimbledon
1998 World Cup qualifiers	4 (Azer, Hun, Swi, Hun)
Goals	1 (Swi)
World Cup finals games	3 (1994 Mex, Ita, Ire)

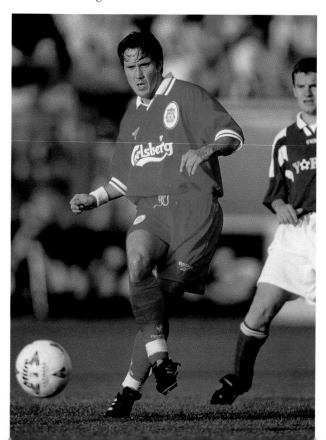

GUNNAR HALLE
LEEDS UNITED

George Graham's fist signing as manager of Leeds and a versatile member of the Norwegian Squad which qualified for France. He had a long apprenticeship in English football with Oldham before moving to Elland Road for £400,000 in December 1996. His tackles always count and his skill and pace are impressive - and, while he doesn't score many goals, he is a major contributor in every game.

GUNNAR HALLE

VITAL STATISTICS

Born	11.8.65. Larvik
Height	5'11"
Weight	11-0
Previous clubs	Lillestrom (Norway), Oldham Athletic
1998 World Cup Qualifiers	4 (Fin - sub, Fin, Azer - sub, Swi)
World Cup finals games	2 (1994 Mex - sub, Ire)

STAALE SOLBAKKEN
WIMBLEDON

Wimbledon do not employ fainthearts and everyone on their payroll is required to do twice the work of ordinary mortals. Solbakken fits the bill nicely. He joined them from Lillestrom for £250,000 last November and, for their modest investment, they acquired an experienced international who fits comfortably into their abrasive way of doing things. Clever technician, tough competitor.

STAALE SOLBAKKEN	
VITAL STATISTICS	
Born	27.2.68. Oslo
Height	5'11"
Weight	11-7
Previous clubs	Ham-Kam (Norway), Lillestrom (Norway)
1998 World Cup qualifiers	7 (Azer, Swi - sub, Fin, Hun, Fin, Azer, Swi)
Goals	4 (Azer (2), Fin, Swi)

PETTER RUDI
SHEFFIELD WEDNESDAY

Rudi is described as "looking like a stick" by David Pleat who signed the tall midfielder from Molde for £800,000 last October. "But" says Pleat, now with Tottenham "he has steel, and the kind of high resolve which most Scandinavians have". Rudi, operating mostly on the left, likes to run with the ball; and his long legs and tight control give him a deceptive edge.

PETTER RUDI	
VITAL STATISTICS	
Born	17.9.73. Molde
Height	6'0"
Weight	11-8
Previous clubs	Molde (Norway), Perugia (Italy)(loan)
1998 World Cup qualifiers	5 (Azer, Hun, Fin, Azer, Swi)
Goals	2 (Hun, Fin)

OLE GUNNAR SOLKSJAER

MANCHESTER UNITED

Only the best are on the Old Trafford pay-roll - and it is a measure of the cherub-faced Solskjaer that United rate him so highly. Alex Ferguson bought him for £1.5 million from Molde in 1996 as "one for the future" but Solskjaer, impatient chap, was United's leading scorer in his first season. He has flick-knife reflexes, quick feet, sly movement, a disregard for gravity and a natural predator's 'nose' for opportunity. Norway's Footballer of the Year.

OLE GUNNAR SOLKSJAER	
VITAL STATISTICS	
Born	26.2.73. Kristiansund
Height	5'10"
Weight	11-8
Previous club	Molde (Norway)
1998 World Cup qualifiers	4 (Azer, Hun, Swi - sub, Fin)
Goals	3 (Azer (2), Fin)

ROMANIA

Students of the World Cup form book will point to the finals of 1990 and 1994 in stressing the serious nature of Romania's title aspirations. In Italy, they reached the last 16 only to lose to the Republic of Ireland 5-4 on penalties. Four years later, they were in the last eight and again went out on a 5-4 penalty shoot-out, this time to Sweden.

Apart from three pre-War appearances, which shouldn't really rate as global contests, their only other finals qualification was in 1970, when they were eliminated at the first hurdles by England and Brazil. England's sole goal by Geoff Hurst recorded their last win over Romania on that occasion, since when they have met five times. They beat England 2-1 in 1980 in a World Cup qualifier, followed by four draws.

"In France, we'll be shooting for second group place at the very least", says coach Anghel Iordanescu. Their inspiration in his third series will be Gheorghe Hagi, cast in the Maradona mould. Eire's Mick McCarthy recalls the 1990 match: "the nearest I got to Hagi was to exchange shirts at the final whistle."

DAN PETRESCU
CHELSEA

Petrescu was a natural right wing-back before the phrase 'wing back' was invented. He tackles sharply and marks and tracks back intelligently but, most of all, he is an improviser, a space-finder, a source of good ideas and the possessor of a useful shot.

Petrescu moved from Genoa to Sheffield Wednesday in the summer of 1994 and, just a year later, joined Chelsea for £2.3 million - and has been an integral part of the London club's remodelling under Glenn Hoddle and then Ruud Gullit. A Romanian regular, with more than 60 caps, who relishes the thought of pitting his ability and experience against England in Toulouse on June 22.

DAN PETRESCU	
VITAL STATISTICS	
Born	22.12.67. Bucharest
Height	5'10"
Weight	11-7
Previous clubs	Steaua Bucharest (Romania),FC Olt (Romania) (loan), Foggia (Italy), Genoa (Italy), Sheffield Wednesday
1998 World Cup qualifiers	10 (Lit, Ice, Mac, Lie, Lit, Ire, Mac, Lie, Ice, Ire)
Goals	4 (Lit, Ice, Lie, Ice)
World Cup finals games	5 (1990 - selected but withdrew injured; 1994 - Col, Swi, USA, Arg, Swe)
Goals	1 (USA)

VIOREL
MOLDOVAN
COVENTRY

There was an international scrabble for the signature of Moldovan whose reputation grew quickly during Romania's impressive progress to the World Cup finals. He could have played in Italy, Germany or Spain - but chose the challenge and rewards of the Premiership. Coventry paid £3.2 million to Grasshopper Zurich, a club record but a realistic price for a 25-year-old with a proven ability to put the ball into the net. Moldovan is a compact and balanced athlete with pace, variety and a wicked finish. He says that Romania deserve more respect than they get - "and the finals in France will give us a chance to prove many people wrong."

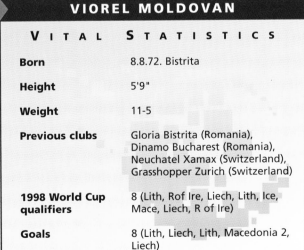

VIOREL MOLDOVAN	
VITAL STATISTICS	
Born	8.8.72. Bistrita
Height	5'9"
Weight	11-5
Previous clubs	Gloria Bistrita (Romania), Dinamo Bucharest (Romania), Neuchatel Xamax (Switzerland), Grasshopper Zurich (Switzerland)
1998 World Cup qualifiers	8 (Lith, Rof Ire, Liech, Lith, Ice, Mace, Liech, R of Ire)
Goals	8 (Lith, Liech, Lith, Macedonia 2, Liech)

SOUTH AFRICA

The emergence of South Africa from the shadow of apartheid has been truly spectacular. Suspended from FIFA in 1964, they remained in exile for 28 years before having their first taste of World Cup football. Then they played four qualifying matches, losing only to the powerful Nigerians who went on to win Olympic gold.

Their hunger for success inspired them to a remarkable 2-0 win over Tunisia in the African Nations Cup Final of 1996 in Johannesburg. Eighty thousand fans urged them to this memorable triumph with cries of 'Bafana Bafana' - Zulu for 'The Boys' - and 12 months later they had won a place in the 1998 World Cup finals. Malawi were beaten 4-0 on aggregate in the first round, followed by 13 points from six games to top the qualifying group ahead of Zaire, Zambia and Congo.

December 1997 brought 'The Boys' down from the giddy heights as they experienced the real world beyond their continent. They garnered but a single point in the Confederations Cup in Riyadh, facing Uruguay, the Czechs and United Arab Emirates. Their disappointed manager Clive Barker resigned, the Frenchman Philippe Troussier took over the reins, and his first great test will be against France on the evening of June 12 in Marseille...a man-sized task for 'Les Garcons'.

MARK FISH
BOLTON WANDERERS

Not many players can claim to have turned down Manchester United. But Fish did, back in the summer of 1996, when the Old Trafford club invited him to have a two week trial. This doughty defender signed instead for Lazio, but eventually regretted it because opportunities were limited with a club which had more foreigners than it could handle - only three could play at any one time. Bolton signed him for two million last August and, despite a knee injury which side-lined him for a month, he has proved a resourceful competitor.

He was at the heart of South Africa's success in the African Nations' Cup and on their long journey to their first World Cup finals. An independent man, even a bit of a hell-raiser once, and he says that the rest of the world will be ill-advised to take Africa's teams for granted.

MARK FISH
VITAL STATISTICS

Born	14.3.73. Cape Town
Height	6'4"
Weight	13-7
Previous clubs	Jomo Cosmos (S Africa), Kaiser Chiefs (S Africa), Lazio (Italy)
1998 World Cup qualifiers	7 (Malw, Malw, Zai, Con, Zai, Zam, Con)
Goals	1 (Malw)

LUCAS RADEBE
LEEDS UNITED

South Africa's captain and one of the best markers in the Premiership - at his best against the best. The fact that he can also play in midfield and has even been an emergency goalkeeper only emphasises that he is a talented chap. He was a league championship winner in South Africa before joining Leeds for £250,000 in the summer of 1994, though he took a little time to acclimatize. He hated the weather in England, spent lonely hours in a hotel and felt worst at times like Christmas. But now he is fully settled, a pillar of Leeds United 's respected defence and, back home, represents the dreams of thousands of kids in places like Soweto...... captain, commanding defender and cult figure.

LUCAS RADEBE	
V I T A L S T A T I S T I C S	
Born	12.4.69. Johannesburg
Height	6'1"
Weight	11-9
Previous clubs	Kaiser Chiefs (S Africa)
1998 World Cup qualifiers	8 (Malw, Malw, Zai, Zam, Con, Zai, Zam, Con)

ERIC TINKLER
BARNSLEY

Tinkler is a strong character who works hard to get his own way in midfield and never seems over-impressed by the quality or reputation of the opposition - just as South Africa won't be in France. But he is not just a big chap who can look after himself. He is tidy on the ball, a discerning passer, makes his mark in set-pieces and is always looking to support the men in front of him.

His experience, too, is considerable. He played for Vitorial Setubal in Portugal for six years and then for the Sardinian club Cagliari in Italy's Serie A before joining Barnsley for £650,000.

ERIC TINKLER	
V I T A L S T A T I S T I C S	
Born	30.7.70. Johannesburg
Height	5'10"
Weight	11-12
Previous clubs	Wits University (S Africa), Uniao Tomar (Portugal), Vitoria Setubal (Portugal), Cagliari (Italy)
1998 World Cup qualifiers	8 (Malw, Malw, Zai, Zam, Con, Zai, Zam, Con)
Goals	1 (Malw)

USA

*S*trange as it sounds, the United States are up there with the stars for their third successive World Cup finals. They are quoted at 150-1 to be 1998 champions. Add two noughts and they might merit a single-dollar fun bet.

They lost all three games in 1990, then qualified for the 1994 finals by footing the bill. Incredibly, they won one of four games on home soil, beating Colombia 2-1 - partly thanks to an own-goal by Andres Escobar, who was shot dead back home two weeks later.

This time they have battled through 16 qualifying matches, finally bisecting Mexico and Jamaica as the three CONCA-CAF qualifiers. But only by defeating Brazil, Germany and Italy to win the World Cup can USA outdim their shining hour - June 29, 1950, at Bela Horizonte, Brazil. Result: England 0 USA 1.

Somewhere, location unknown, that American team is writ in gold letters. Lest we forget, the England team was: Williams, Ramsey, Aston, Wright, Hughes, Dickinson, Finney, Mannion, Bentley, Mortensen, Mullen.

KASEY KELLER
LEICESTER CITY

Keller crosses the Atlantic more often than some Premiership players cross a road. He captained the United States in the 1996 Olympics, is perhaps the most popular 'Soccer' player in America and is now looking forward to being involved in the finals of a World Cup for the third time. He keeps an uncommonly tidy net for Leicester and was one of City's key figures in their Coca Cola Cup success last season.

Keller is a cool and influential 'keeper with safe hands, sharp reflexes and on his day (and he has quite a few) can look unbeatable. His ambition, eventually, is to help promote the game in America.

KASEY KELLER	
VITAL STATISTICS	
Born	27.1.69. Washington
Height	6'1"
Weight	12-7
Previous clubs	Portland University (USA), Millwall
1998 World Cup qualifiers	9 (Gua, Tri, Tri, Jam, Can, CRic, Mex, CRic, Jam)

YUGOSLAVIA

Nouveau Yugoslavia would be a more precise description in the World Cup 1998 programmes. The old country died as a united nation seven years ago with the civil war. As a football nation, they were thrown out of Euro 1992 and 1996 and the World Cup of 1994.

The old Yugoslavia played in eight World Cup finals, reaching the quarter-finals stage five times. Their best year was 1962 in Chile, when they reached the semi-finals in which they lost to Czechoslovakia. They will appear an unknown quantity to two of their 1998 group opponents, never having met USA or Iran in the competition. There are old scores to be settled with the Germans, who lead 4-1 from their five meetings to date.

Surprisingly, although England have played Yugoslavia 14 times they have yet to meet in World Cup Finals. Yugoslavia have qualified for France the hard way, finishing second to Spain above the Czechs and Slovakia. In the play-offs, they slaughtered Hungary 12-1 on aggregate, seven of the goals scored by the Real Madrid hot-shot Predrag Mijatovic.

That the new republic must be taken even more seriously is reflected by their opening odds of 25-1.

DEJAN STEFANOVIC

SHEFFIELD WEDNESDAY

Stefanovic and striker Darko Kovacevic joined Wednesday before Christmas in 1995 in a £4 million deal from Red Star Belgrade. Kovacevic left the following summer for Real Sociedad, but Stefanovic settled happily in Yorkshire and has been a defensive handyman of obvious quality. A diligent marker with a crunching tackle, but also someone with a light touch and a sharp eye for opportunity. He has also scored some important goals.

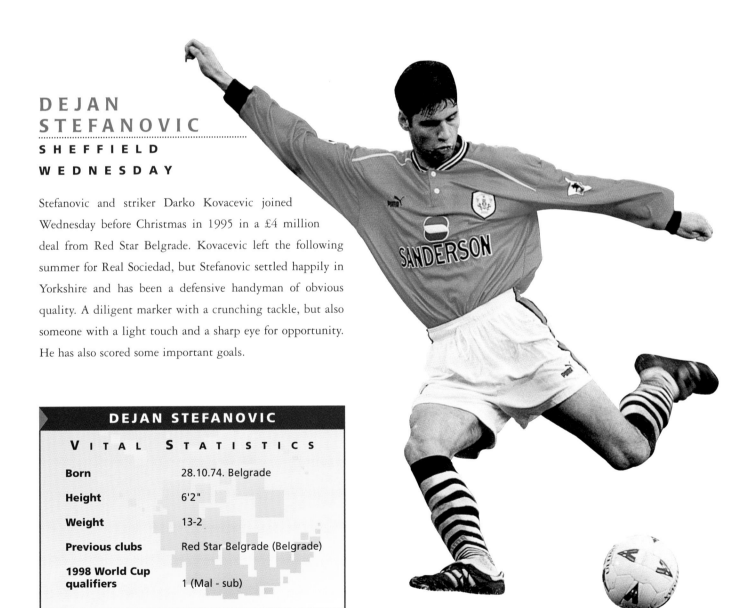

DEJAN STEFANOVIC	
VITAL STATISTICS	
Born	28.10.74. Belgrade
Height	6'2"
Weight	13-2
Previous clubs	Red Star Belgrade (Belgrade)
1998 World Cup qualifiers	1 (Mal - sub)

SAVO MILOSEVIC
ASTON VILLA

Milosevic can be an exasperating chap, as Aston Villa and their fans have discovered, but Yugoslavia certainly have no complaints. He scored some priceless goals on their way to the World Cup finals. Villa bought him from Partisan Belgrade for £3.5 million nearly three years ago - since when he has blown hot and cold, though even on his more eccentric days he is a source of hope. He has that kind of ability, a waspish striker who can sense gaps in the tightest of defensive fences and finish with a heavy wallop or dainty touch. He is a man defenders don't trust but, at the same time, a maverick who can be difficult to accommodate in a team-pattern. His manners, too, are occasionally less than gracious. A spitting incident early in the year put his future at Villa Park in jeopardy.

SAVO MILOSEVIC	
VITAL STATISTICS	
Born	2.9.73. Bijelina
Height	6'1"
Weight	13-8
Previous clubs	Partizan Belgrade (Yugoslavia)
1998 World Cup qualifiers	9 (Far, Mal, Far, Cze, Cze - sub, Spa - sub, Mal, Hun, Hun)
Goals	10 (Far, Mal (2), Far (3), Cze, Mal, Hun, Hun)

THE WORLD CUP FINALS

Will France be changed forever by half a million visiting football fans this summer? Or will these fans be civilised forever by France? One thing is certain: there will be much fun in the sun before we know the answer.

Nine cities, ten grounds; and from industrial Lens in the north, by way of the wine regions, down to Marseilles and Montpellier in the deep south, there will be pleasure and frustration in equal measure. Football, yes, of course, but also problems with tickets, transport and digs against a back-cloth of high security, dedicated profiteering and endless controversy. But most things will work out in the end and there's even a fair chance it could be an outstanding World Cup.

Those who are rich or lucky will get to Paris for the final in the new Stade de France which represents an old dream as well as decades of wrangling and nose-to-tail rows. It is a monument by France to France, built for £260 million (and the rest), a temple of sport which sets standards for the rest of the world.

Only six nations have won the World Cup: Brazil, Italy, Germany, Argentina, Uruguay, (who haven't made the finals this time) and England - and one of them is expected to be champions again. To the winners, the trophy and the glory... to the losers, well, beginning with the Eiffel Tower, there are plenty of high places from which to jump.

Stade De France, St Denis

THE ROUTE TO FRANCE AND THE WORLD CUP

For the first time 32 teams will be vying for the greatest trophy in football. A total of 172 countries entered the tournament and 643 qualifying games were played, over two years - with only France, as hosts, and Brazil, as holders allowed a swift ticket through. There will be 15 European nations competing in France, five from Africa, five from South America, four from Asia and three from North and Central America.

EUROPE

GROUP ONE

	P	W	D	L	F	A	Pts
Denmark	8	5	2	1	14	6	17
Croatia	8	4	3	1	17	12	15
Greece	8	4	2	2	11	4	14
Bosnia	8	3	0	5	9	14	9
Slovenia	8	0	1	7	5	20	1

GROUP TWO

	P	W	D	L	F	A	Pts
England	8	6	1	1	15	2	19
Italy	8	5	3	0	11	1	18
Poland	8	3	1	4	10	12	10
Georgia	8	3	1	4	7	9	10
Moldova	8	0	0	8	2	21	0

GROUP THREE

	P	W	D	L	F	A	Pts
Norway	8	6	2	0	21	2	20
Hungary	8	3	3	2	10	8	12
Finland	8	3	2	3	11	12	11
Switzerland	8	3	1	4	11	12	10
Azerbaijan	8	1	0	7	3	22	3

GROUP FOUR

	P	W	D	L	F	A	Pts
Austria	10	8	1	1	17	4	25
Scotland	10	7	2	1	15	3	23
Sweden	10	7	0	3	16	9	21
Latvia	10	3	1	6	10	14	10
Estonia	10	1	1	8	4	16	4
Belarus	10	1	1	8	5	21	4

GROUP FIVE

	P	W	D	L	F	A	Pts
Bulgaria	8	6	0	2	18	9	18
Russia	8	5	2	1	19	5	17
Israel	8	4	1	3	9	7	13
Cyprus	8	3	1	4	10	15	10
Luxembourg	8	0	0	8	2	22	0

GROUP SIX

	P	W	D	L	F	A	Pts
Spain	10	8	2	0	26	6	26
Yugoslavia	10	7	2	1	29	7	23
Czech Republic	10	5	1	4	16	6	16
Slovakia	10	5	1	4	18	14	16
Faro Isles	10	2	0	8	10	31	6
Malta	10	0	0	10	2	37	0

GROUP SEVEN

	P	W	D	L	F	A	Pts
Holland	8	6	1	1	26	4	19
Belgium	8	6	0	2	20	11	18
Turkey	8	4	2	2	21	9	14
Wales	8	2	1	5	20	21	7
San Marino	8	0	0	8	0	42	0

GROUP EIGHT

	P	W	D	L	F	A	Pts
Romania	10	9	1	0	37	4	28
Ireland	10	5	3	2	22	8	18
Lithuania	10	5	2	3	11	8	17
Macedonia	10	4	1	5	22	18	13
Iceland	10	2	3	5	11	16	9
Liechtenstein	10	0	0	10	3	52	0

GROUP NINE

	P	W	D	L	F	A	Pts
Germany	10	6	4	0	23	9	22
Ukraine	10	6	2	2	10	6	20
Portugal	10	5	4	1	12	4	19
Armenia	10	1	5	4	8	17	8
N Ireland	10	1	4	5	6	10	7
Albania	10	1	1	8	7	20	4

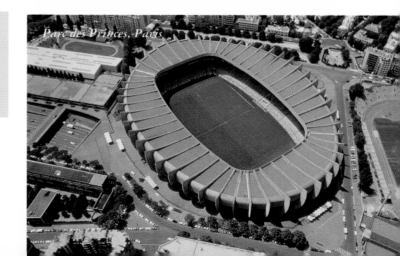

Parc des Princes, Paris

REST OF THE WORLD

AFRICA

GROUP ONE

	P	W	D	L	F	A	Pts
Nigeria	6	4	1	1	10	4	13
Guinea	6	4	0	2	10	5	12
Kenya	6	3	1	2	11	12	10
Burkina Faso	6	0	0	6	7	17	0

GROUP TWO

	P	W	D	L	F	A	Pts
Tunisia	6	5	1	0	10	1	16
Egypt	6	3	1	2	15	5	10
Liberia	6	1	1	4	2	10	4
Namibia	6	1	1	4	6	17	4

GROUP THREE

	P	W	D	L	F	A	Pts
South Africa	6	4	1	1	7	3	13
Congo	6	3	1	2	5	5	10
Zambia	6	2	2	2	7	6	8
Rep of Congo	6	0	2	4	4	9	2

GROUP FOUR

	P	W	D	L	F	A	Pts
Cameroon	6	4	2	0	10	4	14
Angola	6	2	4	0	7	4	10
Zimbabwe	6	1	1	4	6	7	4
Togo	6	1	1	4	6	14	4

GROUP FIVE

	P	W	D	L	F	A	Pts
Morocco	6	5	1	0	14	2	16
Sierra Leone	5	2	1	2	4	6	7
Ghana	6	1	3	2	7	7	6
Gabon	5	0	1	4	1	11	1

Stade Lescure, Bordeaux

Stadium Municipal, Toulouse

SOUTH AMERICA

	P	W	D	L	F	A	Pts
Argentina	16	8	6	2	23	13	30
Paraguay	16	9	2	5	21	14	29
Colombia	16	8	4	4	23	15	28
Chile	16	7	4	5	32	18	25
Peru	16	7	4	5	19	20	25
Ecuador	16	6	3	7	22	21	21
Uruguay	16	6	3	7	18	21	21
Bolivia	16	4	5	7	18	21	17
Venezuela	16	0	3	13	8	41	3

CONCACAF

FINALS

	P	W	D	L	F	A	Pts
Mexico	10	4	6	0	23	7	18
United States	10	4	5	1	17	9	17
Jamaica	10	3	5	2	7	12	14
Costa Rica	10	3	3	4	13	12	12
El Salvador	10	2	4	4	11	16	10
Canada	10	1	3	6	5	20	6

ASIA

SECOND ROUND   GROUP A

	P	W	D	L	F	A	Pts
Saudi Arabia	8	4	2	2	8	6	14
Iran	8	3	3	2	13	8	12
China	8	3	2	3	11	14	11
Qatar	8	3	1	4	7	10	10
Kuwait	8	2	2	4	7	8	8

SECOND ROUND   GROUP B

	P	W	D	L	F	A	Pts
South Korea	8	6	1	1	19	7	19
Japan	8	3	4	1	17	9	13
UAE	8	2	3	3	9	12	9
Uzbekistan	8	1	3	4	13	18	6
Kazakhstan	8	1	3	4	7	19	6

THE ROAD TO PARIS AND THE 'STADE DE FRANCE'

Fill in the blanks and chart the teams progress to provide a record of the tournament.

The first whistle blows on June 10 at 4.30pm, British Standard Time, at Saint Denis in Paris, and for the first time, teams will play their group matches in different stadiums.

In the first round, the top two teams in each of the eight groups will progress into the knockout stages. Three points are scored for a win, one for a draw. In the event of a team being level on points goal difference will be taken into account, then goals scored, then by the result against the competing team.

In the knockout stages, if the games are level after 90 minutes, a 'golden goal' decides the outcome in 30 minutes extra time. If their is no goal the match goes to a penalty shoot-out.

FIRST ROUND

GROUP A
June 10	Saint Denis	Brazil v Scotland
June 10	Montpellier	Morocco v Norway
June 16	Nantes	Brazil v Morocco
June 16	Bordeaux	Scotland v Norway
June 23	Marseilles	Brazil v Norway
June 23	Saint-Etienne	Scotland v Morocco

GROUP B
June 11	Bordeaux	Italy v Chile
June 11	Toulouse	Cameroon v Austria
June 17	Montpellier	Italy v Cameroon
June 17	Saint Etienne	Chile v Austria
June 23	Saint Denis	Italy v Austria
June 23	Nantes	Chile v Cameroon

GROUP C
June 12	Marseilles	France v South Africa
June 12	Lens	Saudi Arabia v Denmark
June 18	Saint Denis	France v Saudi Arabia
June 18	Toulouse	South Africa v Denmark
June 24	Lyons	France v Denmark
June 24	Bordeaux	S Africa v Saudi Arabia

GROUP D
June 12	Montpellier	Paraguay v Bulgaria
June 13	Nantes	Spain v Nigeria
June 19	Saint Etienne	Spain v Paraguay
June 19	Parc des Princes	Nigeria v Bulgaria
June 24	Lens	Spain v Bulgaria
June 24	Toulouse	Nigeria v Paraguay

GROUP E
June 13	Saint-Denis	Holland v Belgium
June 13	Lyons	South Korea v Mexico
June 20	Marseilles	Holland v South Korea
June 20	Bordeaux	Belgium v Mexico
June 25	Saint Etienne	Holland v Mexico
June 25	Parc des Princes	Belgium v South Korea

GROUP F
June 14	Saint Etienne	Yugoslavia v Iran
June 15	Parc des Princes	Germany v USA
June 21	Lens	Germany v Yugoslavia
June 21	Lyons	USA v Iran
June 25	Montpellier	Germany v Iran
June 25	Nantes	USA v Yugoslavia

GROUP G
June 15	Lyons	Romania v Colombia
June 15	Marseilles	England v Tunisia
June 22	Toulouse	Romania v England
June 22	Montpellier	Colombia v Tunisia
June 26	Saint Denis	Romania v Tunisia
June 26	Lens	Colombia v England

GROUP H
June 14	Toulouse	Argentina v Japan
June 14	Lens	Jamaica v Croatia
June 20	Nantes	Japan v Croatia
June 21	Parc des Princes	Argentina v Jamaica
June 26	Bordeaux	Argentina v Croatia
June 26	Lyons	Japan v Jamaica

SECOND ROUND

June 27 Parc des Princes
Winner of Group A v Runner-up of Group B

.... : ....

June 28 Saint Denis (Paris)
Winner of Group D v Runner-up of Group C

.... : ....

June 29 Toulouse
Winner of Group E v Runner-up of Group F

.... : ....

June 30 St Etienne
Winner of Group H v Runner-up of Group G

.... : ....

June 27 Marseilles
Winner of Group B v Runner-up of Group A

.... : ....

June 28 Lens
Winner of Group C v Runner-up of Group D

.... : ....

June 29 Montpellier
Winner of Group F v Runner-up of Group E

.... : ....

June 30 Bordeaux
Winner of Group G v Runner-up of Group H

.... : ....

Stade De Lens, Bollaert

Stade St Etienne

Stade De France, St Denis

Stade De La Beaujoire, Nantes

July 3 Nantes
Winners at Parc des Princes v
Winners at St Denis

.... :

.... :

July 4 Marseilles
Winners at Toulouse v
Winners at St Etienne

.... :

.... :

July 3 St Denis (Paris)
Winners at Marseilles v
Winners at Lens

.... :

.... :

July 4 Lyons
Winners at Montpellier v
Winners at Bordeaux

.... :

.... :

July 7 Marseilles
Winners at Nantes v
Winners at Marseilles

.... :

.... :

July 8 St Denis (Paris)
Winners at St Denis (Paris) v
Winners at Lyons

.... :

.... :

THE FINAL

July 12 St Denis (Paris)

.... :

.... :

3RD PLACE PLAY-OFF
July 11 Parc des Princes

.... :

Stade Velodrome, Marseilles

*Stade Lyons,
Gerlan*

GLOSSARY

Arsenal
Tony Adams (England)
Dennis Bergkamp (Holland)
Martin Keown (England)
Marc Overmars (Holland)
Emmanuel Petit (France)
David Seaman (England)
Patrick Vieira (France)
Ian Wright (England)

Aston Villa
Gareth Southgate (England)
Savo Milosevic (Yugoslavia)

Barnsley
Eric Tinkler (South Africa)

Blackburn Rovers
Lars Bohinen (Norway)
Kevin Gallacher (Scotland)
Colin Hendry (Scotland)
Billy McKinlay (Scotland)

Bolton Wanderers
Mark Fish (South Africa)
Per Frandsen (Denmark)

Chelsea
Celestine Babayaro (Nigeria)
Tore-Andre Flo (Norway)
Ed de Goey (Holland)
Frank Leboeuf (France)
Roberto Di Matteo (Italy)
Dan Petrescu (Romania)
Graeme Le Saux (England)
Gianfranco Zola (Italy)

Coventry
Gary McAllister (Scotland)
Viorel Moldovan (Romania)

Crystal Palace
Attilio Lombardo (Italy)

Derby County
Deon Burton (Jamaica)
Christian Dailly (Scotland)
Jacob Laursen (Denmark)

Everton
Slaven Bilic (Croatia)
Duncan Ferguson (Scotland)
Claus Thomsen (Denmark)

Leeds United
Alf-Inge Haaland (Norway)
Gunnar Halle (Norway)
David Hopkin (Scotland)
Nigel Martyn (England)
Lucas Radebe (South Africa)

Leicester City
Matt Elliott (Scotland)
Kasey Keller (USA)

Liverpool
Stig-Inge Bjornebye (Norway)
Paul Ince (England)
Bjorn-Tore Kvarme (Norway)
Oyvind Leonhardsen (Norway)
Steve McManaman (England)
Michael Owen (England)
Jamie Redknapp (England)

Manchester United
David Beckham (England)
Henning Berg (Norway)
Nicky Butt (England)
Andy Cole (England)
Ronny Johnsen (Norway)
Gary Neville (England)
Phil Neville (England)
Gary Pallister (England)
Peter Schmeichel (Denmark)
Paul Scholes (England)
Teddy Sheringham (England)
Ole Gunnar Solksjaer (Norway)

Newcastle United
Phillippe Albert (Belgium)
David Batty (England)
Alan Shearer (England)
Jon Dahl Tomasson (Norway)

Sheffield Wednesday
Petter Rudi (Norway)
Dejan Stefanovic (Yugoslavia)

Southampton
Egil Ostenstaad (Norway)

Tottenham Hotspur
Frode Grodas (Norway)
Colin Calderwood (Scotland)
Sol Campbell (England)
Jurgen Klinsmann (Germany)
Allan Nielsen (Denmark)
Ian Walker (England)

West Ham United
Rio Ferdinand (England)

Wimbledon
Staale Solbakken (Norway)
Robbie Earle (Jamaica)
Efan Ekoku (Nigeria)
Marcus Gayle (Jamaica)
Neil Sullivan (Scotland)

Published by Stopwatch Publishing Limited

For Bookmart
Desford Road
Enderby
Leciester

ISBN 1-900032-32-5

A CIP catalogue record for this book is available from the British Library

This edition published 1998

The views and opinions of the writers in this book are not necessarily those of Bass Brewers Limited

This is not an official World Cup Book

Based on an original idea by Mike Flynn

Text © Bryon Butler and Frank Nicklin
Photographs © Allsport UK Limited (thanks to Mark & Marc) & Empics, Nottingham

Designed by Ad Vantage (Jon, Carol, Rachel)

With thanks to Chris Rhys for the facts and statistics

Printed and bound by Butler and Tanner Limited, Frome, Somerset

© Stopwatch Publishing Limited
443 Oxford Street, London W1R 1DA
House Editor : Chris Haughton
Production Director : David Brown
Sports Editor : Barrie Gill